# Latin Sayings for Spiritual Growth

**Also by the author**

*Because There Is Jesus: A Call to Be New-Made in Christ*

# Latin Sayings for Spiritual Growth

Archabbot Lambert Reilly, O.S.B.

Our Sunday Visitor Publishing Division
Our Sunday Visitor, Inc.
Huntington, Indiana 46750

Our Sunday Visitor Publishing Division
Our Sunday Visitor, Inc.
200 Noll Plaza
Huntington, IN 46750

ISBN: 0-87973-943-6

LCCCN: 00-140002

Cover design by Tyler Ottinger

Dustjacket cover photos by Mary Jeanne Schumacher,
courtesy of Saint Meinrad Archabbey

Interior design by Sherri L. Hoffman

PRINTED IN THE UNITED STATES OF AMERICA

*Amicus amico:*
For my friend, confrere, and mentor
Gabriel Verkamp,
Sixth Abbot of Saint Meinrad,
who personified and humbly diffused
the wisdom of the ages.
*"Requiescat in pace."*

# Contents

## Part II—Spes

*Sayings That Inspire the Virtue of Hope*

**Part III—Caritas**

*Sayings That Inspire the Virtue of Love*

## Part IV—Prudentia

*Sayings That Inspire the Virtue of Prudence*

## Part V—Justitia

*Sayings That Inspire the Virtue of Justice*

## Part VI—Fortitudo

*Sayings That Inspire the Virtue of Fortitude*

## Part VII—Temperantia

*Sayings That Inspire the Virtue of Temperance*

# Praefatio Prima

(Editor's Preface)

*In Nomine Patris, et Filii, et Spiritus Sancti* were the words that began my mornings at eight for two years from 1980 to 1982 while I was a student at Saint Meinrad College in southern Indiana. My Latin teacher was Benedictine Father Lambert Reilly, who also served as my spiritual director during the same period. Although I was half awake most mornings, the messages communicated during those early classes have stayed with me over the years.

Father Lambert, sensing that I was a "sleepy" student, required that I sit in the front row for his class and frequently called on me, keeping me ever vigilant. On one particular occasion when I did not show up at all, he led the entire class to my dorm room. My roommate let them in while I continued in my deep sleep, roused a few moments later to awaken looking directly into the face of Father Lambert as he conjugated *amo, amas, amat*, the class standing behind him, trying to hold back its laughter.

Although I sometimes experienced the class as a terror, and while I may have forgotten some of the vocabulary, the Latin sayings with which Father peppered his lessons, as well as his spiritual direction, have stayed with me in the years since. I often have found myself either thinking of a particular dictum or even giving voice to one or the other as life has taken me on many varied roads since the Saint Meinrad days.

In 1999 I was hired by Our Sunday Visitor as an acquisitions editor. A short while later I visited my alma mater for Holy Week. While I had been away from Saint Meinrad those many years I found that my Latin teacher had been elected archabbot of the Archabbey of Saint Meinrad. It was he who presided at the Easter Vigil.

While sitting at five in the morning on Easter Sunday in the Archabbey Church, I listened as the archabbot preached in the familiar voice and with frequency quoted Latin sayings that drove home the point of his message.

A short while later I asked Archabbot Lambert to compile a list of Latin sayings along with his own commentary so that others might benefit from his wisdom. Although he was reluctant to do so, I quoted to him his own words, which in turn are the words of Jesus, *Noli timere!* — "Fear not!"

You now hold in your hands the results. Some of the sayings you will recognize. Others, though ancient, may be new to you. The wisdom of each is timeless and will benefit you greatly.

Added to each are the reflections of Archabbot Lambert, who has served faithfully since 1956 as a Benedictine monk. The archabbot has spent his years as a Benedictine both in and out of the monastery. There have been years in parish ministry, giving retreats, others as a chaplain to religious, and there has been a bout with cancer, which has only confirmed his unwavering faith in the Lord.

His wit and wisdom have existed and continue to exert their positive influence on God's Church. May this book extend his ministry even further.

*Deo Gratias!*

*Amen.*

Michael Dubruiel
Feast of St. Meinrad
January 21, 2001

# Praefatio Secunda

(Author's Preface)

Wisdom comes from the ages. We learn when we have to. Sometimes a quick thought can offer a needed meditation, and a short meditation can change one's life. It doesn't really matter who said it; what matters is that it's been said and it's now being heard and accepted.

Over the years, I have studied and taught a bit of Latin. What I've studied and taught has become a part of me. Upon invitation (with a little push), I've agreed to put on paper this little book. If the reflections don't help you, I'm sure the quotations will, if you but stay with them. For the Latin scholars among you, please be warned that many of the translations are not literal, or *de verbo ad verbum* ("word for word"); rather, they have been translated to convey the point or message of the quotations as effectively as possible.

We are called to truth, and as St. Ambrose tells us: Truth from any source is from the Holy Spirit.

There is an old Latin saying, *Discimus docendo* — "We learn from teaching." Ever desirous of being the student, but called upon to be the teacher, I have but a few thoughts coming from my heart and from the lips of earlier and wiser teachers.

As St. Augustine heard and heeded, so I encourage you. *Tolle et lege* — "Take and read." Who knows the good that may come your way?

✠ Lambert Reilly, O.S.B.
Archabbot of Saint Meinrad Archabbey
Solemnity of Our Blessed Father Benedict
July 11, 2000

# Prooemium

(Introduction)

*In medio stat virtus*

("Virtue stands in the middle")

St. Thomas Aquinas

The ancient words of wisdom contained in this small book confront the breadth of human life and activity: love, work, suffering, joy, youth, old age, and death. But as we read and ponder these well-tested truths, one common thread becomes evident: Vice always is rooted in excess or defect of some sort. Virtue, as the words above indicate, stands in the middle.

If I presume on God's mercy, that's too much hope, and my spirit can become bound by pride. With too little hope, I am guilty of despair. If I believe that God loves me, and wants to work with me in my life, then this is the kind of hope we call virtue. So it is with every other aspect of life: If I wish to be virtuous, all of my actions should fall on middle ground.

As we'll see throughout this work, it's clear that the power for virtue and vice is the same power. Where it stands on the continuum determines which it is.

Too much of anything or too little can make one sick. There are those who are always going overboard, and we see in their actions an extremism that is not good. Virtue, what is good for us, lies in taking the middle path.

May your reflections on these Latin sayings lead you to following Our Lord and Savior Jesus Christ every day, always pursuing the middle way.

# *Part I*

# FIDES

## Sayings That Inspire the Virtue of Faith

## *Omne verum a quocumque dicatur, a Spiritu Sancto est*

("All truth is from the Holy Spirit")

St. Ambrose

We can learn something from everyone if we allow ourselves the opportunity. Truth is truth, no matter who says it. As we journey toward God, our eyes must always be open to that Truth, knowing it can be found anywhere and everywhere. Taking on the mind of Christ, we can separate the wheat-word from the chaff-word.

Recently one of the priests of our monastery asked me if I read the writings of a controversial author whose words regularly push boundaries and test faith.

I replied that I thought she wrote well up to a point — the point at which she allows her bias to show.

He said to me, "I'm glad to hear you say that. I like some of what she says, but I can't stand that I do, because so much of what she says I don't like at all."

The words of human beings open to the Holy Spirit give us hints of Truth, but we can never forget something quite important: They're only human. Only God is God. Only God is absolute Truth, trustworthy all the time, any time. ‡

## *Casus non datur*

("There is no such thing as chance")
ST. THOMAS AQUINAS

St. Paul says, "We know that in everything God works for good with those who love him, who are called according to his purpose" (Romans 8:28). Yet sometimes it is difficult to apply this to our lives.

Once my superior said to me, "It's not good for you or for the monastery for you to be stationed here presently."

Those words hurt me and I resented my new assignment away from the monastery. However, with the passage of time I learned there was something I had to learn and would not have if I had remained in the cloister. Praise God for the exile. Now at last I can say thanks for the directive of the abbot and acknowledge the hand of God working through him.

Instead of asking why when something happens and giving voice to the atheist in us, we should ask, "Lord, what do you want me to learn from this?" ‡

## *Festinamus ad Christum, non currendo sed credendo*

("We hasten to Christ not by running but by believing")

St. Augustine

Movement toward Christ involves belief in Him before actual steps are ever taken. In the same way that an infant will take his first steps toward someone he trusts, so too in the life of faith.

Why do we believe anyone about anything? For two reasons: What's told us is possible and the witness is reliable.

Isn't it true, though, that some of what Jesus tells us doesn't always seem possible or even reasonable? "Whoever would save his life will lose it" (Matthew 16:25); "Love your enemies" (Matthew 5:44); "Sell all that you have and give to the poor" (Mark 10:21).

These words are hard to believe at first, but an honest heart sees their truth, and for two reasons: First, living has taught us that letting go, loving, and generosity always bring more peace than grasping, hating, and selfishness. Second, there is the Witness Himself, One whose resurrection from the dead makes Him the most reliable of all.

Faith in the words starts with faith in the Speaker. ‡

## *Quidquid fit, causam habet*

("Whatever happens has a cause")

St. Thomas Aquinas

When something takes place, there is something or someone behind it.

The person of strong faith is able to see that God is behind whatever happens. Nothing occurs except for a reason.

If we believe that God is behind the events of our day we will not take lightly what seem to the unbeliever accidents. Everything has a purpose. Reflection with the eyes of faith searches for the meaning, confident that it can be found.

If God is the cause of every event in our lives, then nothing that happens to us is without meaning. There are no distractions, no intrusions in my day. Rather there are visitations and moments of encounter to be experienced.

If we believe, we will never be tempted to use the excuse of those who say, "Lord, when did we see thee. . . ?" (Matthew 25:44). ‡

## *Numquam minus solus, quam cum solus*

("Never less alone than when alone")

JOHN HENRY CARDINAL NEWMAN

When one is alone, one can invite into his life anyone he wishes.

Alone, we have the opportunity to invite God into the silence. When we open our hearts in faith to that presence of God, we can also do something quite paradoxical. Alone with God, we can tap the reality of any and every person and every situation in the world.

This is why the contemplative life is dedicated so much to the benefit of the world. This is why those behind the walls, so to speak, are so much for those who live outside of them in the world. They invite them in.

We are never really alone when we see with the eyes of faith. If we do not perceive this truth we then need to join the prayer of the two blind men of Jericho, "Lord, let our eyes be opened" (Matthew 20:33). ✠

## *Cantare amantis est*

("To sing is characteristic of the lover")

ST. AUGUSTINE

When one is in love, one can't stand still and keep quiet. One must speak to the beloved. One must speak of him. And sometimes, filled with the love that is too much for words, one must sing.

The Psalms are our love songs to God. Some are attributed to King David, others to unknown figures, all of whom bring forth in their songs all the sentiments, emotions, feelings, and desires that anyone who knows love is able to experience.

It is the Spirit who inspires the lover and it is the lover who sings his glorious dependence on the Lord God in the Psalms, the prayer book of the Holy Spirit.

> But I will sing of thy might;
> I will sing aloud of thy steadfast love in the
> morning.
> For thou hast been to me a fortress and a
> refuge in the day of my distress.

O my Strength, I will sing praises to thee,
for thou, O God, art my fortress,
the God who shows me steadfast love.

— Psalm 59:16-17 ‡

## *Solet hora, quod multi anni obstulerint, reddere*

("One day is sometimes better than a whole year")
Publilius Syrus

A change for the good can take place in our life in a single moment and it's far more than has been accomplished in a long time. What has happened is that God has offered His grace and, at last, we have been open. Then an insight comes and we can't be as we were.

God's grace comes regularly, but necessarily connected with this gift is what Jesus calls *docibiles Dei* — "being teachable of God." People can watch a gift being set down on a table before them. Opening the gift, being grateful for it, and then putting it to use in one's life takes something more.

When the gift of grace is accepted, life isn't like it was before. That moment may be dramatic, as with the vows embraced in religious or married life. Or it may be a glimmer, a whisper, or a thought coming deep in a quiet night that changes everything for years to come because in that single brief moment, we accept the gift with faith in the Giver. ‡

## *Ama Deum et fac quod vis*

("Love God and do what you will")

St. Augustine

At first hearing, these words might sound like the beginning of an excuse. Just love, we might be tempted to think, and the excitement of pure freedom is ours.

But of course, this is not what St. Augustine meant. It is not that we can say "I love God," and be left to whatever comes into our fantasies. Loving God means wanting to share in the mind of Christ and to share His way with others. So the more we love God, the more we do what we will but — and here's the life-giving paradox — since we love God, what we desire will be in line with what God wills.

Love unites and brings us to the same mind and the same will as the one we love. If the love of God is primary and is the first commandment, then we are among those who say, "Lord, Lord"; but unlike those whom Our Lord condemns, we also do what the Lord really wants. ‡

## *Felix, qui nihil debet*

("The happy person is the one who owes nothing")

TRADITIONAL

With a little twist, we can say, "He who goes borrowing, goes sorrowing."

People think they will be happy if they have; so then getting becomes all-important, no matter how. Of course, we know how the story ends, every time: When all that's desired is obtained, what hangs over the acquirer's head are debts of every kind and a collection of toys that will do nothing but wear out, break, and leave us wanting more.

Anything that's acquired has the possibility of loss built right into its joints and shiny surface. That's why Our Lord tells us quite clearly, "Do not lay up for yourselves treasures on earth, where moth and rust consume and where thieves break in and steal, but lay up for yourselves treasures in heaven, where neither moth nor rust consumes and where thieves do not break in and steal" (Matthew 6:19-20).

When we owe no debts to this world, it cannot bring us sorrow. Drawing riches from God and having less of the world's goods is the way to have more, since only the uncluttered mind can see the truth: *Tu autem idem ipse es* — "You, O Lord, are always the same." ‡

## *Mortuo leoni, etiam lepores insultant*

("Rabbits may pull dead lions by the beard")

TRADITIONAL

As we have life, so we are to live it. We are to live it within the call of who God has created us to be. One who knows this — who lives aware of one's limitations as a creature and possibilities as an especially blessed creature made in God's image — accomplishes much.

One who refuses to accept this truth can be overcome by almost anybody. If we lose faith — that is, if we turn our back on God's call to be precisely who we are — then downfall easily will be ours.

The source of Samson's strength was his hair. It was the sign of his dedication to be the person God had called him to be. When Samson succumbed to human voices that demanded he turn his back on who he was, he was overcome. When the hair grew back, he overcame others and himself at the same time in faith. Like the dead lion, unable to threaten its former prey any longer, when our source of strength is gone, we're done for. ‡

## *Pecunia regina mundi*

("Money is the ruler of the world")

TRADITIONAL

Gold is the sovereign of all sovereigns. Like any ruler, gold inspires and motivates. It brings its followers to their knees; it moves them to set all else aside for its own sake; it promises happiness for those who put their lives at its feet.

But for all of us who look for salvation to pieces of metal and what they buy, the day comes when we learn that it's just not possible. Money can't buy peace of mind or hear our pleas for forgiveness and wholeness. In fact, the exact opposite is true. Peace of mind often comes from giving everything away.

All this tells us that the world passes, that there is more to existence than what is here. Faith that's placed in things that rust is wasted faith. As St. Teresa of Ávila says, "We don't build our home on a bridge." ‡

## *Vox populi, vox Dei*

("The voice of the people, the voice of God")

HOMER

The Roman philosopher Seneca said it another way: *Crede mihi, sacra populi lingua est* — "Believe me, the speech of the people is sacred."

Goodness is in God and goodness is in His people. If goodness is in people, then the voice of God comes through them. Earlier, Cardinal Newman, and later, the bishops of the Second Vatican Council spoke of this when they helped us see how important the *sensus fidelium* — the Holy Spirit working through the "sense of the faithful" — is in our growing understanding of God.

It works like this on a more personal level, too. When we want to learn about God, we turn to words and ideas and find them helpful. But in the end, what is the source of our most powerful lessons in faith — words or the lives of others who believe? We know that St. Teresa was right when she said, "In the rough times, show me a man living God's will, so I can truly learn that His Word works." ‡

## *Non bis pueri sumus, ut vulgo dicitur, sed semper*

("We're not children twice, as the saying goes, but we're always children")

SENECA

A Roman proverb expressed the idea that old men are twice children: *Bis pueri senes.* Hundreds of years later, in *As You Like It,* Shakespeare agreed, describing the last act of life as ending in "second childishness and mere oblivion."

But the philosopher Seneca offers us a different idea: We are always children. How can this be?

There comes a time in life when we feel "grown up," but with age we realize that there is still so much that we do not know, so much to learn. We learn that in the realm of eternity we are always children — children of God.

Jesus makes it clear: "Unless you turn and become like children, you will never enter the kingdom of heaven" (Matthew 18:3).

Faith involves looking to God from the point of reality, as a child looks to a parent: in dependence and trust. When it comes to faith, we so-called grown-ups must be willing to be reborn. ‡

## *Quem di amant, adolescens moritur*

("Only the good die young")

PLAUTUS

Some of the saints left this world rather quickly, like St. Thérèse. Some stayed on a long time, like Alphonsus Liguori. Most probably desired to move on and were ready for God's will to be brought to completion in their lives at any time. St. Paul is the one who says, *Cupio dissolvi et vivere cum Christo* — "My desire is to depart and be with Christ, for that is far better" (Philippians 1:23).

When it comes to death, our choice matters little. Long before we ever opened our eyes to His creation, God knew. God knew when we would begin and God knew when we would end.

The shape of our time on earth is unknown to all except the One who made time. Some may fear the mystery, but with the eyes of faith, we trust.

We don't know, but God does, and that is enough for faith. ‡

## *Maria montisque polliceri*

("The promise of the seas and
the mountains")

SALLUST

There is a German saying, "Big in the head and little in the follow-up." Some promises, made in moments of excitement or offered as an extension of our pride, are impossible to keep. Such promises as these are simply beyond the power of the speaker. Do we recall Peter's promises of faithfulness to Christ and his failure to keep them?

God's promises seem the most extreme of all: A child will be born of a virgin. Your sins, no matter how great, are forgiven. Spend your days on earth loving God first, and death will not really be the end.

Wild fantasies? Impossible visions? Not with God, the One who can do anything, the One who can do all things.

With that same God, we can do some impossible things, too. We can be at peace with life as it is, rather than striving for more. We can forgive. We can even love our enemies.

It's all because of faith. In faith, we take on the mind of God, open our hearts to His strength, and live within the peace of His promises. ‡

## *Tempora mutantur, et nos mutamur in illis*

("Times change and we with them")

LOTHAIR

Alexander Pope once said, "Manners with fortunes, humors turn with climes, tenets with books, and principles with times."

We don't live as we used to. We don't build a home and then an outhouse in the backyard. Life on earth changes dramatically, and in some ways, we change, too. We move faster. We take less time to ponder and reflect. In some ways we are more passive, in other ways more active.

Our challenge is to be able to see what doesn't change under the confusion and busyness of what does. God still loves. His Spirit still moves through creation. His Son still stands ready to save.

None of this changes. With the eyes of faith, we see this. With the eyes of faith, we value the beauty and excitement of human creativity, never forgetting that the purpose of it all — giving glory to God — remains always the same. ‡

## *Urticae proxima saepe rosa est*

("The rose is neighbor to the thorn")

TRADITIONAL

That which is beautiful may be dangerous. That which is beautiful needs protection so that harm isn't done to it. That which is worthwhile, one has to pay for. There is, it's said, no such thing as a free lunch.

What is most worthwhile, of course, is love. Anyone who has really loved knows the pain that goes right along with it: watching the beloved suffer, unable to really help. Letting go and watching a child, now almost grown up, walk free into the world.

The joy of the resurrection follows the pain of crucifixion. The beauty and wholeness of eternal life is borne for us out of the suffering of the One who loved. The gift is offered, perfect and undeserved, but never can we forget what made it possible: the Son of God, crowned with thorns. ‡

## *Diem vesper commendat*

("Praise the day at night, and life at the end")

TRADITIONAL

Another way of saying it is, *Nescis quid vesper serus vehat,* meaning, "You know not what the close of evening will bring with it."

No one knows what the future brings. That's why one had better make it a practice to depend on God, in good times and in bad. As Our Lord said: "Therefore do not be anxious about tomorrow, for tomorrow will be anxious for itself. Let the day's own trouble be sufficient for the day" (Matthew 6:34).

There's a civil war going on within us, between the person God has created us to be and a shadow self (the self the world tells us we have to be). We can go either way at any time, toward good or toward ill. God's will should always be our goal.

That's why we should think that if there's good in us, it's God's goodness shared, and not claim too much on our own, as if goodness takes up residence in us because we are who we are. Any self-boasting may well be an indication that we are looking for a reward here and not doing God's will but looking for the approval of those around us.

Canonizations don't take place until *after* a saint's death. ‡

## *Placuit Deo per stultitiam praedicationis salvos facere credentes*

("It pleased God to save believers through the foolishness of preaching")

ST. PAUL (1 CORINTHIANS 1:21)

For any preacher to believe that he's "it" is a complete waste of time. He adds to his preaching whatever are his gifts, and everything is gift. What takes place through the preaching is what the power of God works.

On the other hand, nobody should be so sophisticated that he can't learn from one who doesn't have his wisdom. He has to learn that God is found in the least, and for the hearer it may be that God is found through one who seems less intelligent, whose way of speaking is less than smooth and who stumbles over his words. Moses, we might remember, protested his call because he was not an eloquent speaker. That didn't matter to God. He found a way to work through him.

It's not a matter of the blind leading the blind: *Caecus . . . caeco*. It's a matter of God gracing the speaker and the hearer, and all being open to the Holy Spirit within, no matter what the outer shell looks or sounds like. It's God, God — period. Will we ever catch on? ‡

*Ego sum lux mundi; qui sequitur me, non ambulat in tenebris, sed habebit lumen vitae*

("I am the light of the world; the one who follows me does not walk in darkness, but has the light of life")

JESUS CHRIST (JOHN 8:12)

One doesn't accept these words at face value. One has to have faith that enables these words to sink in with meaning.

So much of life appears dark and unclear, and if we believe that the appearance is all that really is, then we're in trouble. But if we regularly refer our thoughts to the correcting value of the mind of Christ, then we're walking with clarity and precision. Jesus is the light of the world. He lights up the world. He lights up our lives. That light shows the way even when our mightiest powers of reason fail us.

But this is His promise, and believing Him who can do anything, and believing Him who can neither deceive nor be deceived, turns a spotlight on our steps, choices, and decisions that is flashed our way from heaven itself. ‡

*Renovamini autem spiritu mentis vestrae et induite novum hominem*

("Your inmost being must be renewed, and you must put on the new man")

St. Paul (Ephesians 4:23–24)

In so many different ways, this message comes across in the Holy Word. It's an ongoing, unending thought. It's tied to the thought of Newman: "To live is to change, to change often is to have become perfect."

The renovating power is the Spirit and the fount, for it is Christ Jesus. He is the source from whom all good flows. We are to be putting on always that which is good, that which is better. No matter how old we are, Jesus opens to us challenge and promise of newness. "Your attitude," Paul writes to the Philippians, "should be the same as that of Christ Jesus" (Philippians 2:5, *New International Version*).

Another way to think about it is to see that we're all called to a mind transplant, and that Mind is infinite, without end, and so the change is constant, and the change is ever calling us. ‡

## *Quodcumque dixerit vobis, facite*

("Whatever he tells you, do")

The Blessed Virgin Mary (John 2:5)

"Do whatever he tells you," Mary tells the waiters at the wedding feast of Cana. They are the only directive words Mary ever speaks in the Gospels. Words, too, that are always in vogue and always in order. Words that echo the direction from heaven coming from the Father: "This is my beloved Son, with whom I am well pleased; listen to him" (Matthew 17:5).

Words spelled out by one who knows their meaning. Words spelled out from the perfection of Mary's sinlessness. Words that will lead us sinners into the call that we have with Mary. She is the one who says, "Let it be to me according to your word" (Luke 1:38). She is the one who says, "This is the call for all of us. It's yours and it's mine. I have listened and carried it out. You're learning to do the same."

"Whatever Our Lord tells you, do."

*Fides.* Faith. ‡

# *Part II*

# SPES

## Sayings That Inspire the Virtue of Hope

## *Peccatores in re, sancti in spe*

("Sinners in reality, saints in hope")

St. Augustine

We are who we are — flawed creatures seeking grace despite ourselves, despite the world.

If we believe that we're without sin, we're guilty of idolatry, and we've lost our passport into the presence of Christ. If we believe we are helpless against sin, then we've lost the map that will lead us into that same Presence: Hope.

Sometimes our weakness can lead us to despair. Yes, we fall. Yes, forces that make getting up so much harder surround us, forces that celebrate sin and tell us we can never be more than we are.

But St. Augustine offers us a more balanced view. We can't ever forget that we're sinners, but neither can we forget that we have the potential to be saints. With God, all things are possible. As St. Elizabeth Ann Seton said, "Hazard yet forward."

God never gives up hope for us. How dare we think we know better than He does? ‡

## *Imbrem in cribrum gerere*

("To pour water into a sieve")

PLAUTUS

Imagine the sight — endlessly letting the water flow into a container filled with holes. What a useless way to pass time! What a waste!

If we're not careful, our spiritual lives can take a similar turn. We fall into a sinful habit. Before long, we've let that sin control and define us and we've given up on our own potential for holiness. We waste days and weeks moaning that we're beyond hope, that God can never love us, that we can never change.

It's simply not true, and that's exactly why despair is a sin and hope is a virtue. When we insist on pouring the water of our precious lives through the sieve of hopelessness, we're wasting it. We're allowing sin to control us, rather than the promises of God to entice us. ‡

## *Jeiunus raro stomachus vulgaria temnit*

("Hunger finds no fault with
what's given to eat")
HORATIUS

St. Benedict knew that not everybody has the same tastes. He settles this situation gently and prudently when he says, "At the main meal let there be two cooked dishes so that if the monk can't make his meal of one, he can make it of the other."

But sometimes, in the monastery or outside of it, we don't have a choice. We must eat what's in front of us or go hungry.

It's the same with our lives. Life may afford us countless choices, but they all start from the same place: who we are, and we don't have a choice about that.

It was God's decision to make us who we are. The gifts, talents, and even the limitations are the basic ingredients. Spiritual growth is a simple matter of accepting the reality of what God's given us and working with Him in the hope of shaping that self into a reflection of His love. ‡

## *Cor gaudens exhilarat faciem*

("A joyful heart lights up the face")

SALOMO

St. Teresa of Ávila says, "Deliver us from frowning saints!" This doesn't mean that we are to be Pollyannas, blind to the harsh realities of life; but it does mean that in our hearts we know that whatever happens, the Lord is dealing with us as we should be dealt with.

When we realize that whatever we are experiencing is something to help us along the road to eternal life, we can bear it, and we can bear it in hope. That inner hope then finds its way to our countenance, and we'll live the truth that Paul expresses in Romans when he says, "We rejoice in our sufferings, knowing that suffering produces endurance, and endurance produces character, and character produces hope" (Romans 5:3-4).

The joy in our heart that we experience when we realize that the Lord loves us and would never leave us will reflect His light for all to see. ‡

*Omnis agens agit propter finem, saltem virtualiter*

("Every agent acts on account of an end at least virtually")

St. Thomas Aquinas

Whether we're conscious of it or not, St. Thomas points out, purpose guides our actions. If our ultimate purpose is eternal life, then every move we make during the day, great or small, will be powered by that hope.

And if it's not, it shows. As Jesus says, "Where your treasure is, there will your heart be also" (Matthew 6:21). Our lives are mere expressions of where our hope really lies.

Hope is vital to the Christian life because so much of our purpose lies beyond what we can see or understand. "For here we have no lasting city" (Hebrews 13:14). Hope gives us strength to live in peace today, looking forward in trust to the eternal city.

Cardinal Newman says, "There is something that each one of us has to do in this life that no one else can do and if we don't know what it is in this life we will be told what it was in the next." Our end, it's clear, is rooted in our beginnings. ‡

## *Certa amittmus, dum incerta petimus*

("We lose the certain while we seek the uncertain")

PLAUTUS

It's one of the hardest lessons in life: losing what's sure because of the lure of the greener-looking grass on the other side of the fence.

Folk tales turn on the point as well: A man goes far and wide to seek treasure, only to find it at home, under the floor of his very own cottage. Our Lord warns us of setting out in search of many false messiahs that He said would arise.

The Christian's spiritual life can stumble into that trap if we're not careful. We're bored with our ordinary ways of praying, so we look through books filled with the latest spiritual trends, the "newest" ways of thinking about God.

But what happens then? Don't we usually end up feeling much like the spouse who learns that the "flash in the pan" was never more than just that, then gratefully returns home to the one who's waiting faithfully?

Our hope may be in the unseen, but with thousands of years and countless witnesses to guide us, there's nothing uncertain about the journey there. ‡

## *Improba vita mors optabilior*

("A good death is far better than an ill life")

TRADITIONAL

The Day of Judgment will come, there's no doubt. The book will be opened and the record will be at hand. How we have lived and how we have died will judge us.

As we live, we should be growing from whatever point we're at: The bad are to get good, the good are to get better, and the better are to get better still. Good is never good enough because Jesus tells us, "You, therefore, must be perfect, as your heavenly Father is perfect" (Matthew 5:48).

All of this moving forward in hope brings us to the point of transition, the moment of death. If our journey has been made in hope, that moment will be even more hopeful still: repentance of all that kept us from God, and hope that the way is now clear for fulfillment of the promise.

We live with the hope that we, though sinful, will cry out to Our Lord as death approaches and will hear the words that greeted the dying thief who hung on the cross near Jesus, "Truly, I say to you, today you will be with me in Paradise" (Luke 23:43). ‡

*Veritas laborare potest, vinci non potest*

("Truth is able to work, it's not able to be conquered")

TRADITIONAL

Another saying reminds us that "truth and oil are ever above." The oil floats on top of the vinegar, and truth always maintains its own place in our lives, past and present.

So much of sin is rooted in the avoidance of truth. We can't face the truth that strong relationships take commitment, so we try to find happiness the easy way. We want to succeed, but we don't want to admit that success takes hard work, so we cheat and lie our way there. We know that if we face God, we'll have to face the truth about ourselves, and we certainly don't want that, so we stop praying.

But we can't last long that way. The truth may be hard to face, but it's the truth alone that makes us free, and commitment to what's true is the foundation of growing closer to God. Why bother to place hope in anything, if it's not the Truth? ‡

## *Omnia fert tempus*

("Time will tell")

TRADITIONAL

The infant sees nothing beyond her own small fist. The child's vision expands slightly to take in the faces around him and the hills visible beyond his own backyard.

But even the adult can't see the whole picture at any given moment. How many times have we lived in anxiety and urgency for an event to occur, only to look back and wonder what the fuss could have been all about? How many times have we experienced pain that seemed to lead us to the edge of despair, then looked back and seen that same pain as a door to greater wisdom?

Here's a call to caution, then. Don't act too soon; don't judge too quickly, either yourself or others. Life is so rich and complex that it requires time to be understood.

But as far as time can take us, it can never take us to a complete understanding of all that is. God made that very clear to Job.

Our hope ultimately rests, not in our own comprehension, but in trusting that God in His wisdom understands, and that is all that finally matters. ‡

## *Gallus in suo sterquilinio plurimum potest*

("Every rooster is proud on
his own dunghill")

SENECA

We can't do everything.

That can be frustrating sometimes, since there's so much to be done.

But when the fact is simply accepted for the simple reality that it is, it can be a great relief. We don't have to solve everyone's problems; we don't have to fix every single flaw we encounter on the journey.

We're called to do our own part, and that's enough.

As we look around this vast world, the suffering we see can overwhelm us, and our limitations can be frustrating.

But here, as in all things, we're called to trust God. He's given every soul a job to do, every individual talents and gifts to use in one's own little part of the world to make it an ever more beautiful place, ever more reflective of His glory and love.

When we listen carefully to discern exactly what that plan is for us, we're able to grow in faith and hope, strengthened for that task, knowing that it's ours and ours alone.

And like the rooster, then we'll have something to be proud of. ‡

*Nolite timere eos qui occident corpus, animam autem non possunt occidere; sed potius timete eum qui potest et animam et corpus perdere in gehennam*

("Do not be afraid of those who kill the body but who cannot kill the soul; rather be afraid of the one who can destroy both soul and body in Gehenna")

JESUS CHRIST (MATTHEW 10:28)

We live in constant awareness of threats to our physical health. We must quit smoking, we shouldn't drink so much, we should watch our food intake, and we really should exercise more. We are on constant guard against those who could harm us: We lock our doors, stay in safe neighborhoods, and learn all about self-defense. All this is well and good. God gave us bodies that are, as Paul reminds us, "temples" to care for with reverence and gratitude.

But do we protect our souls with the same vigor as we guard against harm to our bodies?

Our greatest fear should not be for somebody who can destroy us physically, but for one who can destroy us forever — one who can tempt us, blind us, seduce us, and be the occasion of our giving up on the Lord and making our way squarely to hell.

As with the saints before us, our hope should be, not in the passing things of this world, but in the unchanging promise of the next. *Quid haec ad aeternitatem?* was the question they always asked: "What's this in view of eternal life?" ‡

## *Noli timere . . . propter quod ego sum tecum . . .*

("Do not fear, because I am with you")

Jesus Christ (Acts 18:9–10)

How many times do we hear these words in Scripture? From Abraham to Moses, to Mary and Joseph, and here, to Paul, they are spoken from the Lord's loving presence.

The world, indeed, is full of terrors — and without hope, we will succumb to them.

But with hope, we are conscious that the Lord is present alongside us in every situation. Not just now and then, not only when we're feeling particularly virtuous, but at every moment.

If He's always with us, then what is there to fear? The Lord is with us, so whatever is, is somehow supposed to be, and whatever's supposed to be, is ultimately for our benefit.

In hope, we live in awareness of God's love, and we drink in the words of Our Lord, "Do not fear, only believe" (Luke 8:50). ‡

## *Spe gaudentes*

("Our joy is in hope")

St. Paul (Romans 12:12)

Where is joy to be found?

Is it in good health? Success? Friends and family?

As we grow spiritually, we come to understand that true joy can't be tied to the present moment. As wonderful as those moments might seem, every one of them can be taken away in an instant, and when that happens, where will our happiness be rooted?

But if our joy is in hope, then our joy is connected, not to what we have, but to what we will have. If our guiding principle lies in looking forward to the eternal happiness to come, then joy can never be lost.

This would be the right way to understand our identity as "Easter people." Our "Alleluia" isn't connected with jumping up and down in the air now because of our present experience. It's a calm realization that what lies ahead exceeds even the greatest joy we can feel in any of our earthly moments.

Let your joy be in hope. This can be one of our greatest blessings and a true directive for the identity of a real Christian. ‡

*Si Deus pro nobis, quis contra nos?*

("If God is for us, who can be against us?")

St. Paul (Romans 8:31)

God has revealed His love for us in the person of Jesus Christ. St. Paul tells us that "neither death, nor life, nor angels, nor principalities, nor things present, nor things to come, nor powers, nor height, nor depth, nor anything else in creation will be able to separate us from the love of God in Christ Jesus our Lord" (Romans 8:38, 39).

Suffering could be added to the list. God does not promise freedom from suffering for His friends. In fact, there's no doubt we will suffer, as Jesus Himself did. "The Cross is the gift I give to my friends," is what the Lord told St. Teresa of Ávila.

Although that which is difficult will be regularly ours, God's sustaining power enables us to conquer in His name, which means through His presence within us.

So here's where our hope lies: If God is with us — and the difficulty is a sign that He is — we can endure and overcome. No enemy has a chance if he is opposing God, and if God is with us, no enemy has a chance to conquer us. ‡

*Elegit nos . . . ut essemus sancti et immaculati in conspectu eius*

("He chose us to be holy and spotless in his sight")
ST. PAUL (EPHESIANS 1:4)

We have been chosen by Christ, and chosen to be holy. Ponder the implications and you will realize that your sanctification is God's will.

There is no success that God acknowledges other than holiness. When we come before the judgment seat of God and are called in, it will because He, the Father, will see in us His Son. He will be seeing the unique being He created and perfected through Christ. We will literally be Christ in a way no one else is capable of being Christ. That's what holiness is.

We do not fear our inadequacies in fulfilling this mission because as St. Paul says, "In him we have redemption through his blood, the forgiveness of our trespasses, according to the riches of his grace which he has lavished upon us" (Ephesians 1:7-8).

So there's our hope: When God made each one of us, He threw the mold away, but He called each one of us in that individuality to take on the likeness that is in Christ Jesus and has lavished us with mercy and love to accomplish that goal. ‡

*Conversi estis ad Deum a simulacris, servire Deo vivo et vero*

("You have been called from idols to God, to serve him who is living and true")

St. Paul (1 Thessalonians 1:9)

Every call has two parts: It is a call toward something and a call away from something else. Another Latin expression tells us, *Terminus a quo . . . terminum ad quem* — "We move from where we are to where we're supposed to be."

The spiritual life is a life of continual self-examination. What is it today that keeps me from God? Whose voices do I heed before I even think of listening to God? What sins am I reluctant to turn from? What parts of me do I keep from God's control?

That's where we are and, as we grow spiritually, we let go; we turn and we move in another direction, giving ourselves completely into the hands of God, where we are truly held. St. Benedict has this in mind when he exhorts us "to prefer no one and nothing to Christ."

It can be frightening, letting go of idols and earthly hopes. But once the idols are shattered and our eyes are free to really see, the hope of God's promise stands clearly, beckoning us to a peace that never ends. ‡

## *Tempus dolorem lenit*

("Time softens all sorrows")

CHAUCER

Most of us know this saying as "Time heals all wounds." Whenever we have a difficulty or an experience of grief, it's necessarily front and center. At that moment, we can't see it within the context of our whole life.

There is no greater mystery we face on earth than suffering. For the person of faith, time softens grief, not merely because it passes and emotions fade. No, there is more for us.

With time, we are able to place suffering in context. We can see how God worked through the suffering to instruct us. We can see how we have grown in holiness, because suffering demanded that we confront life as it is, not as we would like it to be.

And we can place our own suffering at the foot of the cross. There all suffering meets and is offered to God. There all suffering is turned and reborn, as we trust in God's plan and hope in His promise. ♱

# *Part III*

# CARITAS

## Sayings That Inspire the Virtue of Love

## *Caritas prima sibi*

("Charity is first to itself")

JOHN WYCLIFFE

Where does love begin?

The Scriptures offer the answer, simple and profound: "God is love" (1 John 4:8).

God is the source of love. God's love surrounds us from our beginnings, offering us an embrace we are free to accept or reject, filling us with a peace we are free to keep for ourselves and to share.

And what then? God loves us, so whom must we love?

It's not enough to love in general or to profess love for people we never meet. We're not called to love the idea of a person. We're called to love people, as they are, unique and specific brothers and sisters.

The only place to begin, then, is with those around us, as the common translation of this saying instructs: "Charity *begins* at home."

As with every other virtue, love takes practice. We learn how to love by taking small steps of kindness and sacrifice right where we are, with those closest to us. At home, we develop this habit of love, so when we walk out the door into the business of our daily lives, we bring God's love wherever we are and to whomever we chance to meet that day. ‡

*In necessitatibus, unitas; in diversis, libertas; sed in omnibus, caritas*

("In necessary things we should have unity; in chance for opinion we should allow liberty; but in all things we should move in charity")

St. Augustine

The "necessary things" that Augustine speaks of are, of course, the elements of faith that God has revealed to us in Scripture and Tradition: There are three persons in one God; the second person became man; that God-man established a church. We're all held to these necessary beliefs.

But somewhere beyond these fundamentals, the chance for differences arises, as well as the chance for arrogance and ill will. It is, of course, hard to have a strong opinion without being opinionated, but Augustine reminds us that, as children of the same Father walking the same path toward the same embrace of love, we should always discuss differences in a spirit of charity.

This call reaches beyond matters of church belief and practice, though. It's good to reflect on our own family lives and consider if we are, indeed, united in the necessary things and if we deal with our minor differences in a spirit in which love, not pride, shapes our words and directs our actions. ‡

## *Qui me amat, amet et canem meum*

("Love me, love my dog")

St. Bernard

It's hard to love someone and not love what and whom that person loves. Love comes to us because of some kind of attraction, some kind of commonality. If we can't love whom and what the one we love loves, it may be that a tinge of jealousy or only supposed friendship is really at hand. That's because important things that extend to love must be a meeting ground for one who loves another. Doesn't the Lord Jesus tell us that endlessly?

So, it follows that the one whom God loves, we are to love. It is a wide embrace and one that takes special care to include the poor, for as Jesus says, "As you did it to one of the least of these my brethren, you did it to me" (Matthew 25:40).

We might also reflect on what this means for our attitude toward the Church. Augustine says, "Insofar as you love the Church, just so far you have the Holy Spirit." The Church is the Body of Christ. The Church belongs to God. To love God means to love all that belongs to Him, and that includes His

Church. It is not our prerogative to separate what belongs and what doesn't, and then say that we love here but not there.

As God loves, so we are called to love as well. ‡

*Illi poena datur qui semper amat nec amatur*

("Of all pains, the greatest pain is to love but to love in vain")

TRADITIONAL

We are made for love. We desire to be loved and to love. In the absence of love, our spirits wither, our world narrows, even God seems very far away.

We suffer when we are not loved, we suffer when we refuse to love, and we suffer when the love we offer seems to fall on closed hearts. It is more than unrequited romantic love that's at stake here. If love is seeking the best interest of the beloved, then of course, when those we love turn from what is best for them, it causes us pain.

It is the pain of a parent whose children fall from faith, or the suffering we experience when a friend insists on a path of self-deceit and self-destruction. We watch, doing what little we can, with a heart that breaks for the suffering that is bound to follow.

It is the pain that the Lover feels when He cries, "Come, my beloved" (Song of Solomon 7:11), and we the beloved of God turn away, walking the rocky and reckless path into darkness, rather than accepting His faithful embrace. ‡

## *Amicitia, quae desiit, numquam vera fuit*

("Friendship which ends was never true")

St. Jerome

Friendship, as St. Thomas Aquinas notes, is "God's greatest natural gift." Since God is love, any time we encounter love, we are in touch with the presence of God. Such is the case with friendship. Friendship connects us with God.

So, of course, the end of a friendship can puzzle us and even break our hearts.

St. Jerome's words can help us put any sadness we're feeling about the end of a friendship into perspective. If we honestly think back to the circumstances in which our now-defunct friendship grew, what will we see?

Perhaps we'll see a relationship that grew out of need, rather than respect. Perhaps we'll see that one of the friends — maybe it was even us — was more of a taker than a mutual giver of time and attention.

Certainly God worked through the moments of that friendship, however flawed it was. For that we can be grateful. But perhaps we can also learn, and next time form bonds rooted more in real, self-giving love, rather than just need or fascination.

It might also help to remember the saying of my novice master: "You never lose a friend," he would say, "you only find out you've made a mistake." ‡

*Amicitia inter pocula contracta,*
*plerumque vitrea*

("No friendship lives long that
owes its rise to the pot")

TRADITIONAL

Friendship is a type of love and like any love, to become real, it takes time. It doesn't happen at a moment.

There has to be a history as far as friendship is concerned. We have to have known the person in joy and in sadness, both in the vicissitudes of life and its delights.

A casual friendship can begin almost anywhere. Sitting on an airplane, waiting in line, we can strike up a conversation and even share details of our lives. Parents watching their children's soccer games and volunteers working on a project build friendly relationships based on their common experiences.

And then, more often that not, as soon as the plane lands, the line moves forward or the season ends, the connection is severed and the hour-long friendship probably never crosses our mind again.

We can't call anyone a true friend until we can say, "Remember?" ‡

## *Concolores aves facillime congregantur*

("Birds of a feather flock together")

TRADITIONAL

There is a saying we all know: "Opposites attract." What most of us don't know is that's only half the saying. The rest of it is, "insofar as they are alike."

There has to be a likeness to bring friends together in the first place. That's why some people may be golf buddies. They may be prayer partners. The golf and the prayer bring them together. The more they have in common, the more they're truly joined.

In the founding of any great work, co-workers are caught up in the same dreams. When we look at the lives of the saints, we see this time and time again. St. Jerome and St. Paula worked tirelessly together translating the Scriptures. St. Francis and St. Clare supported each other in holy poverty. The list of friends, joined by what St. Francis de Sales called the "bond of perfection" of spiritual love, is a long one.

All friendship begins with common experience. It makes sense that the deeper the experience, the deeper the bond. The truest friendships then, are born out of joining the deepest parts of ourselves: the place where God dwells. ‡

## *Qui non zelat, non amat*

("One who does not really burn,
does not really love")
ST. AUGUSTINE

Our modern world has done much damage to the word "love."

More often than not, we associate love with emotions that ebb and flow or linger with mild, pleasant feelings of momentary compatibility.

But love is more. As the saying indicates, love burns.

It is said by some that love is never without resident jealousy, for real love has attachment, not just interest. The interest that real love has is not selfish: It's a commitment to the well-being of the beloved, at any cost.

Real love is willing, and real love wants to act. The question is posed in Proverbs, "Can a man carry fire in his bosom and his clothes not be burned?" (Proverbs 6:27). Love hurts. That's why we say with St. Paul, "*Caritas Christi urget nos* ('The love of Christ urges us on')" (2 Corinthians 5:14).

Love doesn't sit back, and it's not on the sidelines. Love is in the thick of things, and love doesn't count the cost. Love gives. To know how much, we need not look very far: The Cross tells us all we need to know about love. ‡

*Est oculo gratum, speculari semper amatum*

("The heart's letter is read in the eyes")

TRADITIONAL

When writing of love, poets through the centuries speak of the heart as the place where love rests and of the eyes as the point of entry to read that heart and to decipher for whom it beats.

The Scriptures, written by poets as well, speak of eyes searching the heavens, led by the heart to seek the Lord. It is not just our eyes but our entire bodies and lives that reveal our hearts. This is what Jesus meant when He said, "For out of the heart come evil thoughts, murder, adultery, fornication, theft, false witness and slander" (Matthew 15:19).

No matter what word we speak about priorities, what we do and how we make our way in the world speaks even louder. We may say God's will comes first, that following Christ is most important and that God's love is our source and our goal.

But are we telling the truth? When a choice is called for, when we waver between good and evil, between love and indifference, what do our eyes reveal about where our heart really would like to go?

"Create in me a clean heart, O God, and put a new and right spirit within me" (Psalm 51:10). ‡

## *Post hominum cineres oritur clarissima fama*

("It is safer to commend the dead than the living")

ERASMUS

Time passes. Life on earth ends.

How often do we contemplate the face of one we love in a photograph or in our memories and think, "If only I had told her . . ."

Why didn't we?

Why didn't we let those we love know how much we admired and loved them when we had the chance? What was keeping us from praise? What was holding us back from speaking honestly of our care, concern, and respect? What fear paralyzed us when we were confronted with any beloved child of God in need?

It is worth considering what prompts us to silence. It is worth remembering that God, present in every moment of every day, works through us to love and build others up. It is worth putting aside our pride and our selfish fears.

Love is worth speaking of, and before it is too late, so that this saying need not be true for us. ‡

*Quod oculus non vidit, nec auris audivit, nec in cor hominis ascendit, quae praeparavit Deus iis, qui diligunt illum*

("Eye has not seen nor has ear heard nor has it come up into the heart of man, what God has prepared for those who love him")

ST. PAUL (1 CORINTHIANS 2:9)

An animal senses with the powers that the animal has. A human being thinks with what his thinking apparatus allows. What we're called to be is far greater than what we are now, so the faculty we have now is utterly deficient for evaluating or even imagining what is to come.

Paul — loosely quoting Isaiah the prophet who had said, "From of old no one has heard or perceived by the ear, no eye has seen a God besides thee, who works for those who wait for him" (Isaiah 64:4) — tells us that we don't yet have the faculties to understand what will take place when the fullness of life is ours.

The Lord sees us with a double vision: for what we are and for what we can become. We don't have the power now to see what we can become, so here it is absolutely necessary not to waste time trying to figure the unimaginable. We live, we treasure the gift of life, and we wait for what love beyond all understanding has in store. ‡

*Benedictus Deus . . . qui consolatur nos in omni tribulatione nostra*

("Blessed be God who comforts us in all our trials")

St. Paul (2 Corinthians 1:3–4)

Suffering is a part of every life. But, for the Christian, suffering is never in isolation. Our Lord said, "If any man would come after me, let him deny himself and take up his cross and follow me" (Matthew 16:24). So any suffering that the Lord allows is not just our suffering, but is our suffering with Him. Just as the Father consoled Him and enabled Him to go on in His, so He in turn consoles us and enables us to go on in ours.

Sometimes we look at people who suffer deeply, and we say, "I could never take that."

What we don't understand is that God's love makes suffering — even great suffering — endurable. It doesn't remove the suffering, for we are not robots and God is not a puppeteer. But when we look at Christ, who suffered for no other reason than for love of us, we see what love makes possible, and we endure. ‡

*Hic est Filius meus dilectus,*
*in quo mihi complacui*

("This is my beloved Son, in whom
I am well pleased")

GOD (MATTHEW 3:17)

The heavenly Father speaks only three times in the New Testament. The first is at the baptism, when He says, "This is my beloved Son, in whom I am well pleased" (Matthew 3:17). The second is at the Transfiguration, and God the Father says the same thing, but adds to the first statement: "Listen to him" (Matthew 17:5). The third time is recorded in the Gospel of John and happens in response to Jesus' prayer that the Father's name be glorified (see John 12:28).

The heavenly Father points out Jesus as the one who is all-important. Jesus, in agreement with His heavenly Father, says, "Learn from me" (Matthew 11:29).

It is out of love that this same Father created and sustains us. It is He who, in love, sent the Beloved Son among us in our own flesh, touching, forgiving, listening, and teaching. St. Teresa of Ávila said, "The only mistake we make is taking our eyes off of Jesus."

And why, accepting this gift of love for which we yearn, would we want to? ‡

*Haec est enim caritas Dei,*
*ut mandata eius custodiamus*

("For this is the love of God,
that we keep his commandments")
St. John (1 John 5:3)

It's easy to say "I love," just as it's so easy to say "I'd do anything." The truth of the reality is at hand when our lives match our mouths.

Love is more than emotion and even more than an attitude. A scholastic definition of love says, "To love someone is to will to that person what's good for that person and to provide that good if one is able."

We notice that the definition does not say to provide that good "if it is convenient" or even "if it makes one feel happy." The depths of love move us toward God and toward others, no matter what the cost. A parent might be able to think of many more pleasant ways to spend an evening than tending to a feverish child, but love keeps her at the bedside. Uncomfortable — yes. Exhausted — probably. Resentful — sometimes. But what would we say of the parent who was able to leave that sick child without a second thought, tossing an "I love you" behind as she leaves for an evening out? What would the words mean?

So it is with God. To love God means to trust Him, to trust that whatever He asks is what's best for us, and to act upon it. ‡

*Part IV*

# PRUDENTIA

## Sayings That Inspire the Virtue of Prudence

## *Operi Dei nihil praeponatur*

("Let nothing be preferred to the Work of God")

St. Benedict

St. Benedict speaks of the praying of the Divine Office, now often referred to as the Liturgy of the Hours, as *Opus Dei*, "the Work of God." He lets the monk know that this prayer is the most important aspect of the monk's day. Everything else should be worked around it.

At the very sound of the bell that indicates it is time to pray, the monk should leave his hands disengaged and move on to prayer. St. Benedict encourages the monks to vie with one another in arriving first at the Work of God. This is not intended to encourage competition, but simply to make clear the priority of prayer.

Even if our home is not a monastery, every one of us lives in community: a family, a parish, and a world. We have much that keeps us busy, much that occupies us during our days and nights in this task of maintaining community. But if God does not come first, of what use is the work? Putting everything into perspective with God first — this is really prudence. ‡

## *Cogitationes posteriores sunt saniores*

("Second thoughts are wiser ones")

TRADITIONAL

Prudence is one of the cardinal virtues because it is the acknowledgment that we don't know everything. It's recognition that since human judgment is rooted in limited perception, it must be used with care.

Times can arise in which we must act quickly and on instinct. More often, we don't have to. Most of the time, we have ample opportunity to observe, reflect, and form an opinion before a decision must be made. How many times has our premature judgment of another's character been proven shamefully wrong? How many times have we regretted quick, unthinking choice of words?

A woman once took me to task because the monk who had been the celebrant at Mass all the week she was present never genuflected. The woman waited and watched, and at the end of the week, she offered a tirade against the monk. After she had finished, I told her the celebrant had two knee replacements and was physically unable to genuflect.

For this person, even second thoughts had not been enough. It is well for us to wait as long as we can before we even attempt a judgment. None of us can see the whole picture, but with prayer and deepening faith, we can commit ourselves to opening our eyes as much as we can, letting God show us exactly what it is we need to see. ‡

## *Causa finalis est causa causarum*

("The final cause is the cause of the causes")

St. Thomas Aquinas

Prudence requires having our priorities straight. It means knowing where we come from and where we're going. Without that, we wander without a goal, wasting the precious gift of life on side roads and distractions.

The apple pulls the boy up the tree. It's what he sees; it's what he wants. He is willing to do whatever is necessary to get it. That apple is the first thing in his mind in this project and the last thing in his hand.

For the prudent person, all he sees falls into place around that goal. St. Thomas reminds us that God — the final cause — is the source of all that comes into our lives, one way or another. Rising in the morning and closing our eyes at night, mindful of who caused us to be and who causes us to live forever, has its way of helping us keep things straight.

St. Paul reminds the Philippians rather forcefully: "Work out your own salvation with fear and trembling:

for God is at work in you, both to will and to work for his good pleasure" (Philippians 2:12-13). Sorting out what will lead to eternal life and prioritizing the actions of each day is all-important.‡

## *Habitus non facit monachum*

("It's not the habit that makes the monk")

TRADITIONAL

The same sentiment is expressed regarding another vocation: *Barba non facit philosophum* — "It's not the beard that makes the philosopher." Along with the modern rendering, "It's not the clothes that make the man."

In other words, you can't judge a book by its cover. Or a supposed expert by his or her academic degrees. Or the quality of a thought by how smoothly it is expressed. Or the value of an idea by how amusingly it is presented.

When we are driving, what appears to be a pool of water ahead of us turns out to be nothing more than a mirage. So it is with those who present themselves with some kind of spiritual expertise. If you hear someone give one good talk, make it a point to hear a couple more before you begin to take his words to heart. If a writer strikes you as wise in one aspect of life, don't assume her wisdom is comprehensive. Weigh each idea carefully and take it on its own merit.

Appearances can be deceiving. They can capture our emotions, manipulate us, and even blind us to the truth. The deeper our faith, the less likely it is that we'll be taken in, for we'll be trying to see with God's eyes, not with our own poor human vision. ‡

## *Consuetudine quasi alteram quandam naturam effici*

("Custom is almost a second nature")

CICERO

Shakespeare, in the *Two Gentlemen of Verona*, says, "How use does breed a habit in a man." In life, there is to be a naturalness in doing the important things right, an approach that can come only through the prudent nurture of good habits.

It all begins with God, of course. The vibrant and nourishing spiritual life doesn't just happen. It doesn't simply burst into our consciousness from nowhere and then remain full-grown, untended.

Faith is certainly a gift, but as Jesus tells us, it is a gift like a seed — it must be planted in good soil, first of all, and then nurtured by careful attention and good habits.

We draw closer to God the way we draw closer to any friend: We develop the habit of contact and attention. When we encounter human beings, we nurture the habit of seeing them, not for how they irritate us or differ from us, but how God sees them. When we think and act, we do so, always remembering our own identity as God's child and our own goal of eternal life with God. Throughout the day, we pause, quiet ourselves, and listen, just for those small moments that prepare us for greater intimacy with God later on.

We're ready then, because living in accordance with the will of God, begun as a habit, has now become our second nature. "It's like breathing out and breathing in."‡

*Egregie mentiri potest, qui ex loco longe dissito venit*

("A traveler may lie with authority")

TRADITIONAL

Prudence demands that we be like sentries, ever on the lookout for truth. God, our source and our goal, is the Truth. Why waste our time with anything less?

The trouble is, in a world woven through with sin, truth can be hard to tease out from lies. Although baptized and freed from the personal burden of original sin, we dwell in a world still in its fog. It affects us everywhere we turn — from behind us in the past, from all around us in our culture, and even beckoning ahead of us, in the false goals our society demands we embrace.

The traveler may lie with authority because he is not known where he happens to be visiting. Those who hear him know nothing about his past, and have met no one who can either affirm or deny his claims. They are vulnerable to anything he cares to pass off as truth.

In a way, such travelers surround us. They c into our homes on television and computer screens — voices and faces that seem friendly enough, that speak seemingly reasonable words in appealing tones.

But who are they? What is their agenda? What do they really want from us? Do they really care about us as they try to convince us to buy, believe, and buy yet again? What do we really know about all these clever travelers seeking our souls' loyalty? ‡

*Non omni eundem calceum induas pedi*

("Every shoe fits not every foot")

PUBLILIUS SYRUS

Many times during our journey, we turn to Christ just as the Apostles did and implore, "Lord, teach us to pray" (Luke 11:1).

It was simple when we were young: Utter the memorized words, ask for blessings for all we loved, and drift off to sleep, trusting God's presence the same way we trusted that our mother would be there in the morning, gently shaking us awake.

But as we grow older, life reveals its complexities. Our friendships with other human beings change, just as our relationship with God changes. We turn to a shelf filled with spiritual reading for guidance, and the options stump us. We can meditate, pray the Rosary, go to daily Mass, pray by ourselves or with a group. We can be guided by Thomas à Kempis, Ignatius of Loyola, Teresa of Ávila, Francis de Sales, or Thérèse of Lisieux. One deeply spiritual friend is rooted in Adoration, another in Scripture study, still another in both.

What fits us?

We are each, of course, unique, and God is infinite. He approaches each of us in ways that make sense to us and that will bring us close to Him. If God gives one person the gift of experiencing His presence through a certain style of prayer, that doesn't mean it's the only way that leads to Him.

It's another facet of the virtue of prudence: sifting, testing, and listening, to find the prayer that brings us closest to God. ‡

## *Diu deliberandum, statuendum est semel*

("Deliberation should take a long time; establishment is a one-time experience")

Publilius Syrus

In other words, once it's done — it's done.

A word spoken is more than a set of waves fading into the air. It enters not only the ear of the hearer, but his heart, his soul, and his memory as well.

Actions sometimes have consequences far beyond what we may expect or intend. Ask Adam and Eve, if you doubt it.

So one who is prudent chooses words and actions carefully.

The metaphor may be dusty, but it still holds power and truth: What we do is like a stone tossed into a pond. The ripples expand from that tiny pebble, lapping the shore, pushing reeds aside, even as the rock sinks to the bottom, never to be noticed again except by the curious fish.

God gives us a voice. He gives us the potential to affect others in the present and even from the grave, as our children and grandchildren make their own choices, formed by what we have taught them and how we have formed them.

So let us speak carefully, and treat others with care, mindful of the trust God has given us. ‡

## *Profecto deliramus interdum senes*

("The head gray, and no brains yet")

TRADITIONAL

From the time we are born, and perhaps even the months before, we learn.

Every part of us is necessary for this education. Our senses, our minds, and our spirits all play their own part.

Will has something to do with it also. We do not speak as often as we used to of "will," but as St. Augustine and others remind us over and over again, it is the key to any kind of spiritual growth. We may see all kinds of things. We may hear, we may learn. We may even know perfectly well what is right, what is wrong, and what is best for us.

But if our will is not in God's hands, the learning has little use. It sits within us, undirected and purposeless.

Parents scold their children for stubbornly committing the same wrongs over and over: "When are you ever going to learn?" they ask. They wonder how the child can be so dense: He's been punished for the offense, he suffers ill consequences, but still he persists.

We complain about God's mysterious ways and even His seeming absence, but the truth is that God works within the fabric of our lives constantly. He guides, He speaks, He pushes, and He clarifies.

If God never stops teaching, yet we still insist on blundering along, ignoring Him, perhaps it is time to take an honest look at our willingness to be taught.

Will we ever choose to learn? ‡

## *Omnia qui temptat, nil apte perficit umquam*

("One who tries everything perfects nothing well, ever")

TRADITIONAL

Another way of saying this is the well-known phrase "Jack of all trades, master of none."

Life is vast, with seemingly unlimited choices. In such a world, how is one supposed to know which is ours to follow? There is a time for trying things out, for shopping around and testing different possibilities. But the time comes for all of us when we have to stop shopping around and then settle in.

But how will we know?

We start by understanding that this is not merely a practical question. It is a spiritual question as well. God has given us years to spend upon this earth of His. How are we to spend that time? What are we to give?

So that's how we start. We look at our wealth of choices.

And we understand that God has created each one of us with particular gifts and we are to use them.

We have a particular call to fulfill. Cardinal Newman says that there is something each one of us has to do in this life that no one else is called to do.

God isn't keeping it a secret either. It's there if we but open our eyes and try to see with His. ‡

## *Adulator propriis comodis tantum studet*

("One who fawns looks out only
for his own benefit")

TRADITIONAL

Another way of saying it is, "Dogs wag their tails not so much to you as to your bread."

Prudence requires a realistic view of human nature. Of course, we are to think the best of all we meet. We are to treat them as our brothers and sisters in Christ.

But the truth is, as we live and breathe, the reminders of our fall trail behind us, surround us, and sometimes even lead us. This is the world we must live in: a world in which we may be deceived, taken advantage of, and led astray.

One of the greatest pitfalls we can face is allowing our sense of self to be dependent on what others think of us. We believe that our worth derives from being respected at work or within the community. We think that if certain people think well of us, we must be okay and our lives must have a purpose.

But what happens when that moment of acceptance or even brief glory passes? What happens when the funding stops, a new boss comes in, or a new, more interesting face comes on the scene?

We learn the truth then. It wasn't our unique inner selves that were valued. It was something else, something totally replaceable.

The prudent person recognizes this. He sees the world and its honor for what it is and rests his sense of self on the much simpler, enduring, and trustworthy fact that God loves him. ‡

## *In sinu gaudere*

("To laugh up one's sleeve")

Cicero

It is hypocrisy of which we speak here: saying one thing, knowing it is false, and further, taking joy in the deception.

Prudence requires that we be careful in our judgment of others. It is a tightrope we walk between unfair, premature judgment and an unquestioning trust that is easily taken advantage of.

But we might also take time away from our concerns with other people and consider the ways we laugh up our own sleeves.

Even at God, perhaps?

What is the purpose of our spiritual life?

Is it to fit in with a certain community or social expectation? Is it to fulfill a minimal obligation in order to assuage fear about eternal life?

Do we go to Mass, listen attentively, then walk out the door and spend the rest of the week placing worldly goals at the center of our lives, rather than the Gospel?

Could our prayers even sometimes be uttered in order to hand a small gift to God, hoping He won't notice what we're taking with the other and what exactly we are concealing behind that well-worn sleeve? ‡

## *Non omnis, qui nobis arridet, amicus est*

("Not everyone who laughs with us is a friend")

TRADITIONAL

Other English proverbs flow from this saying: "Beware of fawning creatures and their treacherous ways" and "He covers me with his wings and bites me with his bill."

It is certainly true that we can be deceived deliberately by those who want to take advantage of us.

Just as harmful, though, are the supposed friendships we pursue that may be filled with laughter and a certain level of pleasure, but are, in the long run, not in our best interest.

There are times in which the circumstances and combination of personalities in a friendship lead us to be less than we are, less than we should be. We all know that it is easier to sin with a companion. Alone, we have less to distract us from the voice of conscience. The presence of another can give us strength to ignore that voice completely and plunge into wrongdoing, no matter what it is: cruel gossip, destructive activities, or simply shoving God to the side.

We know that true friendship is a gift from God because it brings out the best in us. So now, prudently, we examine our friendships. Do they bring us closer to God or push us away?

The question is: Who are our true friends? ‡

## *Surdo fabulam narrare*

("Tell the story to the deaf person")

TERENCE

We use the expressions "You might as well speak to that post" or "It was like talking to a wall."

As we grow spiritually, our understanding of our role in creation deepens. We shed the foolish illusion that we are in absolute control of life and embrace the will of God with gratitude.

This letting go has many fruits. One of these fruits is that we learn, sometimes painfully, how to use our words prudently.

Jesus sends us all into the world to bear the Good News. When we accept Christ, this is the mission we accept: In every word, gesture, and action, we are to embody His love and share it with all we meet.

Sometimes this love requires us to be silent.

We may speak to and lecture the errant child until our voices are hoarse. But then the day comes when we realize, with a great shock, that his life is not ours. It is his own and he must live it, responding to God's voice within, completely on his own terms, not on ours.

It is not that we do nothing. We continue to love those around us who seem to be making mistakes. It is simply that prudence requires us to catch on when God has finished using our voices and would like us to simply step aside and allow Him to do His work. ‡

## *Fida terra, infidum mare*

("Praise the sea, but keep on land")

TRADITIONAL

Somebody has expressed the same thought in a slightly different way: "Love the sea? I dote on it — from the beach."

The spiritual life involves balance. God moves within us in sometimes startling ways. There is not a model of spirituality we can look to who did not take risks.

Abraham left his homeland behind in obedience to God's voice. Saul led a secure life persecuting Christians until he was knocked off the security of his horse and had to see the world in an entirely new way. From St. Augustine to Dorothy Day, we see a steady trail of figures following the Lord's will in ways that disrupted, confused, and shocked.

But not everything that calls us to break from the past or change our ways is from God. We can easily be fooled. Our needs and pain at any particular time leave us quite vulnerable to the one who uses everything in his power to appeal to our weakness in his eternal cause of drawing us away from God.

So here is the challenge: to be ready to follow God's will in whatever strange directions it may lead, but to be prudent as well, knowing that the sea is deep, wide, and full of shimmering dangers. ‡

## *Pedibus compensanda est memoria*

("A forgetful head makes a weary pair of heels")

TRADITIONAL

The cook who has her ingredients ready before she turns on the stove has a much easier time of it than the one who must bustle about the kitchen, opening boxes, measuring, chopping, and cleaning all at once. The teacher who doesn't plan spends more time on discipline than instruction. The shopper who heads to the mall without a list on the day before Christmas is bound to lose his holiday spirit by dusk.

We can waste a lot of time vainly spinning our wheels, not only in the practicalities of life, but in our spiritual lives as well.

We think that because we are unique and our sense of God is so personal and lies so deep within, that we are completely on our own when it comes to prayer. We flounder and wander, thinking that no one else can help, that no one else can understand our particular challenges.

It's just not so. Not one of us is the first person alive to seek intimacy with God. Millions have gone before us, and innumerable others have written about their journeys. Fellow friends of the Lord in our own parishes and homes surround us.

Their stories, their experiences with prayer, can be of great value to us. In forgetting the gifts our fellow Christians have to offer, we make our solitary journeys all the more weary. ‡

*Part V*

# JUSTITIA

## Sayings That Inspire the Virtue of Justice

## *Quod tibi fieri non vis, alteri ne feceris*

("What you do not wish to come to you, don't do to others")

LAMPRIDIUS

This is the virtue called justice: giving others — both God and neighbor — their due.

We develop this virtue in the same way as we do the rest: by getting into the habit of living it. It begins with this most simple of reminders. If you don't want to be treated in a certain way, avoid that behavior yourself.

The Lord says the same thing positively, "As you wish that men would do to you, do so to them" (Luke 6:31).

We are confronted with this option many times every day, especially when it comes to that most crucial area of the spiritual life: sin and forgiveness. Jesus teaches us to pray, "Forgive us our trespasses as we forgive those who trespass against us" (see Luke 11:4) How often does that challenge greet us throughout the day?

So to others the best!

Then to ourselves as a result, the best! ‡

*Qui petit alta nimis, retro lapsus ponitur imis*

("One who seeks high things too much,
has a fall that goes way down")

TRADITIONAL

Our Lord says, "Every one who exalts himself will be humbled, and he who humbles himself will be exalted" (Luke 14:11). The popular version of this is: "The bigger they are, the harder they fall!"

Justice involves giving others their due. First among "others," of course, is God.

We did not give ourselves the talents we have. We didn't create our own minds, souls, and imaginations. We didn't purchase our ability to love from a catalog.

Every bit of the good that we do is rooted in God's power, not our own.

It's easy to forget this, though. If we're not careful, our pride can prompt us to forget not only that God gave us these gifts, but their divinely intended purposes as well. We can quickly end up twisting Jesus' encouragement for us to "Let your light shine" to "See my light shine!" It's a subtle difference, but powerful.

Using our talents as if they're ours alone may take us to high places in this world, but when we stop and look around, we might be surprised — shocked — at how far we've traveled from God.

It is all gift and the credit all goes to God, not to us. "O Lord, not to us, but to thy name give the glory" (Psalm 115:1). ‡

## *Finis legis non est lex*

("The purpose of the law is not the law itself")

St. Thomas Aquinas

Considerations of justice naturally lead to law.

The human response to law is usually of two kinds: We're grateful when it protects us and resentful when we're restricted by it.

So it is that when we confront Church law or the expectations attendant on membership in a religious organization, sometimes we chafe. There are times in which we might even try to set up enmity between spirituality and religious institutions.

For indeed, Paul tells us that in Christ, we are "discharged from the law" (Romans 7:6). So what are we to make of these Church rules and laws that pop up at us from the Sunday bulletin before Lent begins and in the pre-Cana booklet we're handed when we approach the parish for the sacrament of matrimony?

As St. Thomas reminds us, the purpose of the law is always beyond the law. Ideally, human beings would always be filled with love, be ever anxious to give honor to God and respect to one another, and ready to leave self behind.

But if we're honest, we know that the ideal often glimmers only faintly behind the fog of our selfishness, indolence, and arrogance. We sometimes need the push of obligation to get us to the place where we know we should be anyway: on our knees, sacrificing, tending to souls other than our own, giving honor to the One who gave us life in the first place. ‡

## *Deïecta quivis arbore ligna legit*

("When the tree has fallen down, lots of people go to it with a hatchet")

TRADITIONAL

It's true, isn't it? Just as we tend to avoid responsibility for the bad, we're somehow always ready to take credit for the good, even when we had little to do with it.

The principal of a school or the pastor of a parish receives credit and accolades when the institution succeeds. Much more briefly mentioned are all the teachers and volunteers of every kind who form the foundation of the success.

Perhaps a good but risky idea has finally been brought to fruition. How many times have we said, on such an occasion, "Oh, yes, that's what I thought we should be doing all along"?

We're on all sides of this: We sneak into the light shed by others' good deeds and try to bask in the glow. Then we have the gall to be upset when, in a different situation, other people take credit for the hard work we've done.

Remember that Scripture says, "Your reward is great in heaven" (Matthew 5:12). Two men often do the work and many appear on the scene to get the applause. So what? It all works out; it's leveled in the sight of God, who is, of course, ultimately responsible for all that's good. ‡

## *Qui non laborat, non manducet*

("If you don't work, you don't eat")

St. Paul (2 Thessalonians 3:10)

An old expression puts it this way: "No mill, no meal."

As much as we chafe against it, as much as we'd all rather be sitting by the pool reading a book, as much as we'd prefer a day of leisure to one of work, we know that life simply can't be that way.

Not only does justice demand that we take care of ourselves as soon as we are able and not expect others to provide while we relax, it's also true that when we're constantly served rather than engaged in serving, we remain emotional infants.

What's true for the physical necessities of life holds true for the spiritual life as well.

Because we know that God is everywhere, we sometimes think that our relationship with Him should be as effortless as breathing in the air around us.

We're shocked when we find it's not. We might even resent it and wonder what God is up to.

But the fact is, no relationship is easy. It takes time and effort to get to know another person. The greater the effort, the more we work at honesty, openness, and the simple skill of listening, the closer we get to another, and the deeper our friendship grows.

To be deeply nourished by God requires openness to Him, a task that's a bit more challenging than opening our lips to take a breath of fresh air. ‡

## *Consuetudinis magna vis est*

("The rule of custom has lots of weight")

CICERO

Before one changes a custom, it's good to know the circumstances in which the custom was established and what its purpose is.

Certainly in the monastic way of life, custom is extremely important. As ages roll by, it finds itself modified and sometimes it finds itself cancelled out; but changes are never made without a lot of thought and respect for the original purpose that should be retained, if now in new form.

Custom forms us and establishes us. G. K. Chesterton referred to tradition as the "democracy of the dead" — that is, we who happen to be alive now don't have all the answers. Those who have walked the earth in generations past have much to teach us, and we are fools to ignore their wisdom. One might even call the unthinking rejection of custom an injustice, since in a way, when taken too far, it's an attack on the integrity of those who established it and offer it to us from the past as a gift.

Browsing the shelves of the "spirituality" section in a bookstore, one is struck by the "new" trends that appear with regularity, promising to reveal "contemporary" ways of relating to God. One examines them carefully, wondering what they know that St. Teresa or St. Francis de Sales didn't say first, and more eloquently.

Like so much, it's all about balance: We shouldn't be the first to change, nor should we be the last to hold on. ‡

## *Qualis dominus, talis et servus*

("Like master, like servant")

PETRONIUS ARBITER

Most of us have all sorts of people under our care.

We have employees whose paychecks we sign. We supervise departments. We teach classrooms full of children and young people. We lead ministries and organize volunteers. We have families who are formed in the years spent in our care and under our influence.

Are we aware of how much responsibility we hold?

No leader's control is absolute, nor should it be, of course. Children will do what they like — some will learn and some won't. We may have titles of leadership, but it is the energy of all involved that makes the wheels go and new ideas come to fruition.

But our leadership does do something important: It sets a tone.

A leader who's secure in himself and respectful of others will produce a different environment than one who is narrow-minded and threatened by his co-workers' talents.

A parent who treats her children as gifts from God runs a different kind of household from one who views her offspring as property or as extensions of herself.

It all comes down to this: Any leadership we are blessed with comes from God. Mindful of that, we turn to lead others as the Master has led us: in love, as a servant. ‡

## *Necessitas dat legem, non ipsa accipit*

("Necessity knows no law")

Publilius Syrus

In other words, necessity gives the law; it does not receive it.

This is rock-bottom thinking about justice.

We spend much time today defending our rights and our property. We resent those who would question our right to every brick, every piece of fine china, and every stock certificate in our possession.

"We've earned it," we say. "It's ours."

Justice, we think, demands that we build a fence around what we say belongs to us. Let others work harder, we say, if they want what we have. That's all it takes.

That is, to be sure, some kind of justice. But is it God's?

Jesus told a story about a rich man who felt the same way. He was secure in his claim to his possessions, and saw no reason why this pest named Lazarus should expect anything from him. After he died, of course, and saw Lazarus at Abraham's side, far distant from his own discomfort, he saw things differently.

When we grow in our sense of God's justice, our clenched fists open, the walls come down, and we understand the generosity to which necessity calls us, and its name is justice. ‡

## *Quod cito fit, cito perit*

("What comes on the scene quickly,
quickly perishes")

TRADITIONAL

My grandmother used to say, "Quickly toothed, quickly with God."

No matter how long our life is, it isn't long. We strut the stage for only a short time. The only time we have is the moment we're in.

Wherever we look, we see that which was once new is well on its way to being old, or has already arrived there.

That's why when we catch on to the meaning of life, we should let its meaning direct our every move.

We can't waste time thinking that when life gets better, then we'll have time for God. We can't continue putting off doing the right thing until it's more convenient. We can't keep living for worldly goals, believing that we'll have all the time in the world to straighten ourselves out later.

Because, as we eventually find out in startling, and even tragic, ways, it's simply not so. We may have many things, but there's one thing we don't have: all the time in the world. ‡

## *Alea iacta est*

("The die is cast")

PLUTARCH

God calls us to nourish the virtue of justice in our lives. That means that we are intent on seeing the world with God's eyes, allowing Him to work within us to restore the harmony of creation. It means that we live in awareness of the glory and gratitude that is due God and the love and concern that is due our neighbor.

It also means that we understand that as we sow, so we reap. If this is the way we live, this is the way we are. If what we do leads to a particular goal, then the goal-setting gradually becomes a goal obtained.

In other words, when we choose to turn from God, that is exactly the place our choice takes us: our eyes and ears more focused on some transitory idol, our hearts divided.

God doesn't go anywhere, of course, but since He made us free creatures, there is only so much He can do and still respect our integrity and freedom.

We shouldn't be surprised then, when the steps we've chosen to take have led to a terribly lonely place.

They were our steps: It was where we determined we wanted to go. If we've decided that's the sort of justice we want, why should we be surprised when it's exactly what we get? ‡

## *Quaere adolescens, utere senex*

("The young person seeks,
the old person enjoys")
TRADITIONAL

At times, the busy years of youth and beyond can be a blur.

Our lives turn on an endless cycle of sacrifices and duty: We bear children, provide for them, teach them, support them in grief, and rejoice with them in success. We cannot even start to count the diapers and the long nights of fevers and sickly tears.

We work our intellects hard to understand mysteries. As we move through adulthood, we are stumped by the strange, tragic ways of our world, and there are times our faith is challenged almost beyond belief.

We work hard, we think hard, we bear many burdens for the sake of others. We change our lives, not necessarily because we want to, but because other people need us to.

They are seeds we're planting, and if we're focused on God, they're exactly the right kind of seeds that give us hope for a future of peaceful rest.

The time comes when we can look back, content because we have no regrets. We've been faithful to God, lived for Him and those He's entrusted to us, and now, as He promised, He will be faithful to us. ‡

## *Errare humanum est, ignoscere divinum*

("To err is human, to forgive divine")

CICERO

The first part of this saying is often quoted while the second part is often conveniently left off. The erring is easy to acknowledge; the call to forgive is not.

Our Lord instructed his disciples, "Whenever you stand praying, forgive, if you have anything against anyone; so that your Father also who is in heaven may forgive you your trespasses" (Mark 11:25). This can be termed as one of Our Lord's hard sayings. Hard because it seems almost humanly impossible to fulfill.

Human beings fall; they make mistakes and sometimes they just outright choose to do evil. Sometimes the level of a crime can lead one to say that the act was "inhuman," but most of the time we almost expect human beings to fail and do what they do.

When it comes to us, ourselves, we are usually able to understand why we sinned or why we failed and that gives us the courage to expect forgiveness.

But what about when it comes to those who sin against us? Often this takes a superhuman ability to understand and forgive.

This is justice in the kingdom of God: to forgive those who have sinned against us. To realize that if we do not, we only punish ourselves because we then remain the unforgiven sinner. ‡

## *Absens haeres non erit*

("The person who is absent won't be the heir")

TRADITIONAL

Of all the odd things that we human beings do, one of the oddest is turning our back on what we know is true.

We all want peace. We all want to know why we're here, where we're going, and what the point of life is. Experience, tradition, centuries of wisdom, and Jesus Himself tell us where all of that will and won't be found.

Happiness won't be found in accumulating wealth and possessions.

But we just continue doing it, hoping the next pay raise, the next promotion, and the bigger house will make us happier than we were before.

Yet the questions remain.

It won't be found in putting ourselves and our own emotional satisfaction first. Jesus tells us over and over again that "happiness" and "blessedness" are rooted in loving God and neighbor before all else.

We listen carefully, weigh the options, and then simply continue on our well-worn road, relegating

God to Sundays and our suffering neighbor to the back of our minds.

And then we wonder why we're restless and unhappy, why the peace we think we deserve isn't ours yet, why God hasn't fulfilled His part of the bargain.

As I said — it's an odd thing: to turn one's back on what God tells us will bring us happiness, and then expect to inherit it anyway. ‡

## *Cogitationis poenam nemo patitur*

("Thoughts are free from toll")

ULPIAN

Words — those bits of sound traveling on air from our mouths to another's ear — have tremendous power.

Words have the power to heal and to wound. They can free us and lock us in spiritual prisons. Even as they fade into the air, their echo can resound in a soul forever.

That is why they must be used carefully. It is perhaps why Benedict tells us that it's better to be silent than to speak.

In this world that God has made, everything is related, everything has consequences.

When we speak, we should be ready to pay for what we say, to be prepared for how our words affect others.

The question justice prompts us to ask is not, "What would I just love to say to him?" but rather, "What does he really need to hear from me? What's necessary for me to say and what's not?"

In other words — how does God want me to use this gift of speech today? ‡

## *Deridens alium, non inderisus abibit*

("The mocker doesn't go away unmocked")

TRADITIONAL

We live in an age of irony. Nothing, it seems, is to be taken seriously, and certainly nothing is beyond the reach of mockery.

Satire and poking fun have their place, but when the tone of ridicule and contempt hijacks an entire age and literally nothing is sacred, something is very wrong.

When we nurture the virtue of justice, we're aware that everything that God created has a divinely ordained purpose. We human beings may, in some ways, be ridiculous and hapless creatures, but when the laughter fades, here we stand: beloved children of God.

How do we deal with the flaws and foibles of those around us? Are they reasons for judgment or fun? Do we make any attempt to understand why people are the way they are or do we take the easy way out, blithely criticizing?

The question is, do we treat others as human beings or as objects for our amusement or sense of superiority?

And what happens then, when we look in the mirror? What has treating others unjustly, as less than human, done to our own humanity? ‡

## *Canis sine dentibus latrant*

("The dog without teeth does the barking")

Ennuis

Perhaps you've heard it put another way: "Barking dogs seldom bite."

How effortless it is — to fill the air around us with complaints. It's a convenient way to draw attention to problems without actually doing anything about them.

You may have noticed, in fact, that the louder the complaints, the less likely it is you'll find a soul ready to do the hard work necessary to fix the problem.

Is that really all God calls us to, though? Circling a problem, throwing words at it, then walking away?

Justice calls us to action, not just words.

Justice calls us to open ourselves to God, see the world as He intended it to be, and, energized by His Spirit, work to bring that image to birth.

So, confronted with a problem, here's the question we might ask about our reactions: If it's worth complaining about, surely it's worth fixing. And if it's not really in need of fixing — what are we complaining about? ‡

## *Potest ex casa magnus vir exire*

("A great man can come from a hut")

SENECA THE YOUNGER

Our Lord was born in a cave. Not too far from the monastery where I reside is the boyhood home of Abraham Lincoln — a small log hut. Both can teach us the lesson of Seneca the Younger's saying.

We often make judgments in our lives based on someone's background and where he comes from, unfortunately to our detriment.

When the Apostle Nathaniel first heard of Our Lord and where He was from, he said to Philip, "Can anything good come out of Nazareth?" (John 1:46).

The response of Philip was, "Come and see" (John 1:46).

He did and as a result he encountered God-made-Flesh.

Our Lord warns us about discounting those whom the world rejects. He tells us that we too might encounter him in the person of those we count among the least. Our judgment is not to be as the world judges but rather as Christ does.

The truth is that everyone coming from anywhere is somehow Christ coming from everywhere. ‡

## *Semel malus semper praesumitur malus*

("One who once deceived is always suspected")

Traditional

Aristotle said in a similar fashion, "A liar is not believed when he speaks the truth." This is a dangerous saying. If it's applied literally, then there's not much hope for any one of us because we all fall.

Cardinal Newman says, "To live is to change. To have changed often is to have become perfect."

Human justice holds grudges, is hard on the sinner, and is slow to forgive. Human justice asks proof of repentance and never quite manages to forget the sin. Our human memories hold on to past hurts for a long time, ever ready to revive them in a moment of anger.

Human justice speaks of the leopard who cannot, of course, change his spots.

But God's justice is another matter, for it is a justice woven with eternal mercy and divine love.

Our stories are filled with figures who have, indeed, changed. They, in fact, are people we remember most vividly: St. Paul, St. Augustine, St. Francis of Assisi, St. Ignatius of Loyola, Thomas Merton, and Dorothy Day.

Like the father of the prodigal son, God waits with open arms, knowing that we can change, ready to fill our now-open hearts with the grace that will take us from deception and suspicion to integrity, wholeness, and peace. ‡

## *Mors non accipit excusationes*

("Death doesn't accept excuses")

Traditional

One might ask of a difficult acquaintance: Why should I attempt to be kind to him? Why should I give him the benefit of the doubt? Why not return evil for evil?

We can frame our answer around one single reality: death.

Death will not hear a denial, and death doesn't observe our timetable. Mortality and the eternity beyond have a way of putting the rest of life into perspective.

That's why St. Benedict says to keep death daily before our eyes and desire it with all spiritual longing. That's why the saints are those who judge possibilities and choices by asking, what's this in reference to eternal life?

If anyone thinks he's not going to die, all he has to do is wait to be proven wrong. It is our common fate, just as the Fatherhood of God is our common origin. With that ever behind and before us, what sense does it make to spend the time we have fostering misery and difficulty? What possible reason would there be not to cooperate with grace and give others their due?

If we knew we were going to die today, we would change things.

Perhaps this then means we should change things. ‡

# *Part VI*

# FORTITUDO

## Sayings That Inspire the Virtue of Fortitude

## *Omne initium difficile*

("Every beginning is difficult")

TRADITIONAL

Another way of saying this is, "A good beginning is half the battle." When something new comes our way, fear is often its companion.

It doesn't matter if the moment is something we've hoped and worked for. We know that plenty of unknowns lie beyond the classroom door on that first day of school. Strangers — friendly, but still strangers — greet us as we begin our new job. Our newborn infant fills us with hope and joy, but even so, the nights can be quite long and the worries almost overwhelming.

But we remember. We remember that none of the joys of later life comes without these difficult beginnings. The same hand that writes beautiful poetry once long ago struggled to form simple letters on a writing tablet, afraid he would never get it right. As he puts the finishing touches on a painting, the artist remembers the fears that paralyzed him weeks or months before, as he studied the empty canvas.

We are afraid because, deep down, we know that we are really not in control. We have our plans and our hopes as we begin something new, but if we've been paying attention to life, we know that our plans are usually meaningless, and that's frightening — even though we know that God's plans are far better than anything we could ever come up with! ‡

## *Omne commodum cum suo onere pertransit*

("No pain, no gain")

Nicholas Breton

In the modern world, many tasks are easier than they used to be. Pioneers took months to cross the country; we wing it in a day. Machines wash our clothes and our dishes without our hands getting a bit wet. Food sits quietly on grocery store shelves, waiting. We hand over some pieces of paper to a cashier and walk out with a bag of what our great-great-grandparents had to plant, harvest, and preserve with their own hands.

Yes, life is easier in some ways, but certain truths remain. Most of us may have our basic needs provided by others now, but the work left for us to do is still vital.

The children we raise, the young we teach, the sick we nurse, and all the many works of our hands depend on our willingness to sacrifice, perfect, and stretch our energy and imaginations far beyond our ordinary comfort zones.

God has graced us with the potential. He has gifted us with the energy and possibilities. And He strengthens us to endure the difficulties so that we may do what's right and do it well: *Esto laborator et erit Deus auxiliator* — "Be the laborer; God will be the helper." ‡

## *Semper fidelis*

("Always faithful")

U.S. Marine Corps Slogan

If you are familiar with the military, you've probably heard the saying "Semper Fi," short for *Semper Fidelis*, the U.S. Marines' slogan for "Always Faithful." The Christian is called to no less.

Faithfulness means trust. The question might be raised, trust in what?

Trust in my own abilities? The government? The people around me?

Outside of the cloister at Our Lady of Gethsemane Monastery in Kentucky we find the words "God Alone" inscribed in stone. This is the answer to whom we should trust, not only for the Trappists who live within the walls of that monastery, but for every person on the face of the earth.

Everything else only matters as much as we trust in God alone. And trusting is not a one-time proposition but a lifetime pilgrimage. Like the Marines who may be true to the Corps throughout their lives always proudly greeting one another with a *Semper Fi*, so should the Christian be *Semper Fidelis*, "Always Faithful." ‡

## *Ex improviso subvenit ipse Deus*

("It is always darkest just before the dawn")

THOMAS FULLER

In the order of creation, we know this is true.

The welcome rebirth of the day is almost upon us when the darkness is at its thickest.

Sometimes we apply this to life by considering difficulties and remarking, "Well, it can't get any worse" or "Things can only get better." And that might be true sometimes: Just when we think we're up against a wall, a savior intervenes and light reveals a new, better day.

But there's another way to look at this, too. In those dark nights of the spirit, when loneliness seems to be our only friend and all of our efforts to bring light into a situation have failed, we can't forget that we're really not alone.

The night may seem dark, but a light glimmers faithfully, if we but take our eyes off our misery and look.

God is there when we don't think about Him. He's there when we keep Him in mind. He's there when we expect Him and He's there when we least do, offering strength for the taking to take one more step toward the dawn. ‡

## *In amaritudine salus*

("In bitterness there is salvation")

TRADITIONAL

Cardinal Newman says, "The cross stands and the world revolves around it." Jesus has invited us into suffering as He has invited us into salvation and resurrection. There is no cross-less Christianity. We all have to take our turns carrying that cross, very often like Simon of Cyrene — unwillingly! But then, of course, we learn from what we have suffered; paradoxically, our pain has become a blessing.

It is difficult for us to see this sometimes. We're so accustomed to tying our faith in God to how comfortable we are at any given moment. We decide we're sure of God's love because we're well-fed and well-housed and everything is going our way.

But isn't it foolish to call "blessing" only that which agrees with our thinking? When we look over what we have suffered, we may readily say, "I wouldn't want to suffer it again." Yet how many of us would be willing to give up the lessons learned out of the experiences of such suffering? How much weaker would we be without them? ‡

## *Aliud est facere, aliud est dicere*

("It's one thing to say something,
it's another to do it")
TRADITIONAL

What does it take to speak? A thought (or not) — the slightest exhalation, quick movements of a few muscles. Sound is produced. Words are formed.

And then what?

Jesus tells us many times of the limited value of words. "Not everyone who says to me, 'Lord, Lord,' shall enter the kingdom of heaven, but he who does the will of my Father who is in heaven" (Matthew 7:21).

No, it does not take much out of us to speak. It's easy to preach on the ills of the world. Listing the faults of others takes no effort. Saying that we're Christian is as simple as pronouncing our names.

But what about doing it?

Acting on our words takes something else, and we call that virtue fortitude.

How many times today will the opportunity present itself? We see what must be done. We declare that it must be done. But will we take that extra step, hold fast to God for strength, and actually do it?

Will we? ‡

# *Carpe diem*

("Seize the day")

HORACE

Most people are familiar with this Latin saying from the movie *Dead Poets Society*, which came out some ten years ago. The teacher (played by Robin Williams) at a tiny all-male New England prep school encourages his English literature students to take the advice of Horace and to *carpe diem*, "seize the day." The saying and the teacher turn the quaint and quiet school upside down.

Sometimes we can fall into a rut, where each day becomes a monotonous routine. We get up, go through our daily runs, come home, and go to bed. Hardly a moment captures our interest. How unlike the disciple of Christ who is told by Our Lord: "Take heed, watch; for you do not know when the time will come" (Mark 13:33).

If we take the words of Our Lord seriously, every moment of every day is a potential moment of visitation. We will be ever vigilant for His coming into our lives, ever watchful for His movements in our lives around us. No day is without meaning and every day is a day to truly seize and engage, as Providence unfolds it. ‡

## *Crux est generis omnis*

("The cross is for every race")

Traditional

The cross is the promise of the Lord to His followers. It's what really aligns us with Him.

It is tremendously tempting to misunderstand the purpose of the spiritual life, or even life itself. Our instinct correctly hints to us that we are born to be "happy."

But what does that mean?

If we're not careful, we will absorb our definitions from the world, and we'll strive for that kind of happiness. We'll direct our lives toward material comfort and physical pleasure. We'll even try to judge how much God loves us by how much He allows us to avoid suffering.

We thank God, like the Pharisee, for not making us poor.

We thank God that we're not sick like the other fellow or grieving like the woman down the street.

But that will not be the end of it. It can't be. Our cross will come. In fact, we all carry crosses constantly, no matter if we admit it or not. The burden of our past sin bears on us all the time, affecting our judgment and controlling our choices.

The cross does not discriminate, for Christ does not discriminate. "There is neither Jew nor Greek, there is neither slave nor free, there is neither male nor female; for you are all one in Christ Jesus" (Galatians 3:28). ‡

## *Bos lassus fortius figit pedem*

("An old fox will find a shelter for himself")

TRADITIONAL

When we're young, we know no limitations.

We think we can do anything; we think our mortal lives cannot possibly end.

And we believe we can withstand any temptation just by a combination of self-generated willpower, luck, and unfailing common sense.

The young person tells his mother not to worry about the party: He's strong, he won't do anything wrong. A newly married couple believes their love will be effortless to maintain.

Age and difficult experiences correct our youthful pride. Our mistakes and failures teach us that we are foolish to depend too much on ourselves, and to think everything good will come to us just because we're our own invincible selves.

We learn, eventually, that there are times when it is good to take shelter and not insist on placing ourselves in the thick of the storm to prove ourselves.

Certainly, with God's help we can develop the virtue of fortitude to saintly levels, but is it really necessary to place ourselves deliberately on the precipice?

It's good to get to know ourselves well. It helps to know our limits, and to understand that there are certain situations that easily bring out our worst, and to avoid these situations — these occasions of sin — as much as we can.

And that, of course, takes a bit of fortitude as well! ‡

*Nascentes morimur, finisque ab origine pendet*

("In birth, we are dying, and our end hangs on our beginning")

MANILIUS

A birthday is nothing but our death begun, a march to the grave. The moment we begin to live, we begin to die, and we have here no lasting city.

The road is long and difficult. We are conceived with God's image within us, born with a deep yearning for love and completion.

But that image within us is not what it should be, and there lies the difficulty of the long road ahead for the newborn child.

It takes great strength of spirit to see through the lies that the world tells us about who we are.

When we look ahead down the road from birth to death, we see much that dissuades us from nurturing our true selves. The other voices are so powerful. The sacrifices will be tremendous. Who knows what we will have to let go of along the way?

And it is such a long, long road. How will we know that in the end, our forbearance of all these difficulties will not be in vain?

We may know what we should do, but actually living the right choices takes an act of will. This requires faith. This requires fortitude. ‡

## *Experientia est magistra rerum*

("Experience is the best teacher")

Roger Ascham

Practical wisdom is learned only in the school of experience, and more often than not, these experiences are difficult ones.

Is there any lesson worth learning that doesn't come through difficulty, sweat, and even a little pain?

A mother says that she didn't know anything about love until she bore her own child. But how did the child come? Only through discomfort and pain.

A long-married couple smiles at the idealistic newlyweds, and then says a prayer. The husband and wife know that the road ahead will be filled with mysteries, questions, and challenges, but that the love gained is far deeper and richer than what they shared on their wedding day.

It is easy to say our prayers when life presents no difficulties. In fact, it is so easy it often slips our mind altogether.

Our friendship with God, like any other friendship, deepens as the result of all kinds of experiences:

We learn of His graciousness in surprising blessings. We learn of His faithfulness in difficulty. And we learn how much we really need Him in dark nights when He seems absent.

In the end all experience brings us to the cross. For the Christian the promise of the resurrection leads us like Mary Magdalene to recognize Our Lord in the garden of the empty tomb with the cry, " 'Rabboni!' (which means Teacher)" (John 20:16). ‡

*Quod natura dedit, tollere nemo potest*

("That which is bred in the bone will never come out of the flesh")

TRADITIONAL

St. Thomas Aquinas reminds us that the supernatural doesn't destroy nature; it perfects it.

God creates us as unique creatures, possessed of countless gifts and qualities. It seems that these qualities are present in some form from the beginning. Any parent can tell us that a child hasn't changed much since he or she was born. The quiet one reading in the corner was always quiet, even as a baby. The most restless of the adolescent children roused himself and his parents several times a night through toddlerhood. There is something about our essence that seems to be there from the beginning.

It's not that we can't change. We can. But through our natures, God has given the essential building blocks of who we are. He's given us our natural qualities, but He's also given us something else: His image.

We are perfected by presenting ourselves as we are to Christ. Without Him we are slaves to our fallen nature, but with Him we are new. As St. Paul said, "If any one is in Christ, he is a new creation; the old has passed away, behold, the new has come" (2 Corinthians 5:17). The gifts are the same, but the way we use them is to be for the better. ‡

## *Qui timide rogat, docet negare*

("The one who asks faintly, begs a denial")

SENECA

There is a similar saying by John Gower: "A faint heart never won a fair lady." The thought is the same: If we really want something we will be persistent.

We wonder: Why should God care? He has billions of souls to be concerned about, most with far more serious problems than ours. Surely He has better things to do than listen to us.

According to Jesus, who should know, He doesn't. Jesus lets us know over and over again that our prayers to the Father are not in vain. We, as mere human judges and parents, respond to the needs of those coming to us for help. How dare we think that God would do less?

But then again, Jesus reminds us that strength and confidence must be a part of our prayers. He commends those who dare to approach Him from the back of the crowd, offering their needs to Him, trusting that He will answer. He tells us to go to the

Father over and over, to never stop letting God know what we need.

Praying this way requires all kinds of strength. Fortitude builds our patience. It undergirds our persistence even in the face of the unknown. Above all, it requires taking a great leap of faith.

We ask firmly because we believe God will answer! ‡

## *Nullus difficilis cupienti labor*

("No labor is difficult to one desiring it")

TRADITIONAL

When the will is willing, the feet are light. What's difficult for one is easy for another because desires differ so much. St. Teresa of Ávila reminds us: "Insofar as you desire, you will possess." When the desire is strong, then the will becomes strong and accomplishment is quite possible.

So often we look at others who have accomplished much, and we wonder, "How could they do that? That's far beyond me."

But the fact is, they could be looking at us and saying the exact same thing.

There are challenges associated with any task: The physician must immerse himself in the horror of disease. The accountant lives in a blur of numbers. Parents sacrifice their personal lives for little bundles of need.

But if they are following the call deep within, planted by God, the difficulties are nothing. They fade in contrast to the spiritual unease that comes from giving one's life over to something that might seem physically less challenging, but is unsatisfying and far from fulfilling the nature we've been given.

So we listen carefully, discern where God wants us to go, and because He's the One calling, the strength to proceed is ours. ‡

## *Lapsus semel, fit culpa, si iterum cecideris*

("It becomes a fault if you fall again")

Publilius Syrus

Another saying puts it more concretely: "He who stumbles twice over one stone deserves to break his shins." An even more modern rendering has it: "Fool me once, shame on you; fool me twice, shame on me."

We're supposed to learn from our mistakes. Cardinal Newman tells us: "We learn to do right from having done wrong." In a way, we go into heaven backward.

Our lives are filled with unfortunate patterns, many learned as children, watching our elders. We learn to cope in unhealthy ways. We learn that being loudly negative gets us more attention than being quietly docile. We get a strange satisfaction from making mistakes, and it's difficult to break free.

Because of these habits, so deeply ingrained, we're tempted to say, "That's the way I am. I can't change." That, of course, is never true. It requires will and the strength of God within, but we can change.

A basic principle of morality is that knowledge begets responsibility. When we learn something's wrong, we're not held to what went before retroactively, but from the moment of learning, we're held.

An encounter with the Truth may lead to a pardon but carries with it the command "Do not sin again" (John 8:11). ‡

*Parvula despiciens, conquirit maxima nunquam*

("The one who despises the little things never is able to add up the big things")

TRADITIONAL

There's the saying "The person who will not stop for a pin will never be worth a pound."

We're not born with all of our virtues intact and ready to withstand anything and carve great roads through this world's jungle of temptations and distractions.

The potential is certainly there — we are created in God's image, after all — but the potential awaits our nurture. Cooperating with God's grace, we spend our lives drawing closer to Christ and closer to who we truly are.

But the baby can't even get his fist into his mouth for weeks. The toddler must toss the ball over and over before he masters the simple game of catch.

And so on the inside, we are born with the desire for God burning brightly within us and the paths to Him open and clear.

The virtues that build our souls must be nurtured little by little, in the smallest ways, before we can begin to confront the major obstacles the world presents to us on our way to God.

If we don't develop them in little ways, we'll simply collapse.

As St. Thérèse would say: "There is great grace in picking up the pin from the floor." ‡

## *Estote ergo vos perfecti, sicut et Pater vester caelestis perfectus est*

("Be perfect, as your heavenly Father is perfect")

JESUS CHRIST (MATTHEW 5:48)

The heavenly Father is God. He can't be better.

You and I can be better all the time — so much so that we can grow in goodness until we die.

The very word "perfect" comes from two Latin words — *per* ("through") and *facere* ("to make"). Perfect, then, means that we're made all the way through to what we're supposed to be.

We're not there yet. The journey requires constancy and fortitude.

The perfection demanded of us by Christ is only possible with His help. It becomes our constant goal to be united with Christ. St. Paul who as a Pharisee had longed to master perfection found that in Christ alone he could be made perfect.

This is our goal too, so that in the end, we are able to say with Paul, "It is no longer I who lives, but it's Christ who lives in me" (Galatians 2:20).

When that Father who is perfect can see Christ made in and through us, then perfection will be ours. And on the day of days, we hope to hear Him say: "Come in; I see my son in you." ‡

*Part VII*

# TEMPERANTIA

## Sayings That Inspire the Virtue of Temperance

## *Mens sana in corpore sano*

("A sound mind in a sound body")

JUVENALIS

The balance between body and soul is something that is in the news a lot today. More and more scientists are discovering that there is a link between what we think and believe, and how our bodies react to all this. This is not so much a discovery as a confirmation of what the ancients knew centuries ago.

There is a harmony between what we believe and how we act. There is a connection between what I do on my knees and how I experience the events of the day. If one is neglected, the other suffers.

Often we worry about our bodies but neglect our souls. Our Lord counseled otherwise, when he told His disciples, "Do not fear those who kill the body but cannot kill the soul; rather fear him who can destroy both soul and body in hell" (Matthew 10:28). The body is an expression of the soul and ultimately what we do with the soul truly determines whether we really care about our bodies. ‡

## *Fortiter in re, suaviter in modo*

("What you do, do forcefully
but do gently, sweetly")

TRADITIONAL

How is the Christian to make his way through the world?

When Jesus' words "To him who strikes you on the cheek, offer the other also" (Luke 6:29) are understood wrongly, we might be misled into thinking that Christians are called to weakness.

That's simply not true. Jesus frequently reminds us that those who put God first are to be strong in faith, unyielding in principle, and unafraid to live and express the truth.

But temperance calls us to be attentive to our tone.

The reason is that when we speak without thinking and listening, we're placing ourselves in the center of the conversation, rather than letting God work. Any effect our forcefulness might have is undermined by our lack of love for others.

If we speak overbearingly, without listening, we're guilty of self-centeredness. We can say all we want about God, but if our tone is not compassionate, our words fall flat, expressive of nothing but our own ego.

Jesus spoke the truth with force, clarity, and authority. But He also healed the wounded, forgave the sinner, and welcomed the outcast into His embrace. As François Mauriac wrote, Our Lord "crossed every threshold and sat at every table."

And His words had power, for they were clearly spoken out of love. ‡

## *Simul iustus et peccator*

("We're at the same time just and sinful")

St. Augustine

There is an old saying: "There is so much good in the worst of us and so much bad in the best of us that it behooves none of us to talk about the rest of us."

The Church doesn't canonize anyone so long as the person is alive. Until the last moment of any life there is the potential to sin, as well as to repent.

The bad have to get good and the good have to get better and the better have to get better still because at each stage, there is fault and there is goodness. We can't let the sin in our lives define who we are, nor can we rest easy on our virtues and think there's no room for growth or improvement.

We're created in God's image. Sin has corrupted that image, but as we cooperate with God's grace, the image is restored — gradually, step by step over a lifetime and beyond. ‡

## *Ne quid nimis*

("Nothing in excess")

TERENCE

When good is too much, it overwhelms us and it ends up not being for our benefit at all. We see this in terms of our bodies. Food and drink are intended to nourish and energize us. When we overdo either, we become sluggish and slow. Our capabilities are diminished, not enhanced, as they should be.

When we get or seek too much of anything, we bring disorder into our lives. We're filled, but with the wrong things. We've trained ourselves to be selfish and take what we don't need, possibly depriving others in the process.

Another saying reminds us: *Nauseam copia parit* — "Excess brings about nausea."

This nauseous fruit of excess is harmful, not only to our bodies, but to our spirits as well. For when we are suffering the consequences of selfish overindulgence, our thoughts focus on ourselves and our own discomfort, turning us from the call to put the love of God and others first. ‡

## *Ex peccato peccatum nascitur*

("From sin, sin comes")

Traditional

We sometimes speak of being disposed to do something, and we contrast it with being in the habit of doing it. If we're "disposed" toward a certain behavior, that means we'd like to do it regularly, but we're not there yet.

This applies to all kinds of qualities, both positive and negative. The virtuous person becomes so because of a lifetime of good habits, and, of course, practice makes perfect. It's the same with sin. Once we offer our hand to sin, sin willingly becomes our traveling companion.

When we recall our most stubborn sins, we remember that when temptation struck us many years ago, the first step to sin was agonizing. The second step was less difficult, and sooner than we thought, what was once sin became a necessity or was even transformed into a supposed good deed!

When we develop the virtue of temperance, we grant the various aspects of life the priority appropriate to each. We understand that giving sin even the slightest priority over the good sets us on a road that, if we thought about it seriously, we really wouldn't want to travel. ‡

*Fortuna vitrea est;*
*tum quum splendet, frangitur*

("Fortune is like glass; the brighter the glitter, the more easily broken")

Publilius Syrus

The thicker the glass, the less the sun pierces through. The thinner it is, the more brilliant does it transpose the sun's rays.

The thinner it is, the more it is to be desired. But it is also the glass with which we must take more care. It is the more fragile; it is the one we might find would be best to simply leave alone.

It's true that we're drawn to that which is brilliant. But we need that which is substantial. The promises of fortune can lead us to make foolish choices and decisions. The glitter can fool us, but it never securely situates us.

The person who lives the virtue of temperance understands that God's promises are not waiting far away in another land. God lives here and now; God's embrace is waiting here and now.

When we turn from the excesses of fancy, our eyes are open to see God in the simplicity of the present moment, in the reality of life as it is now, not some glittery, breakable fantasy. ‡

*Nihil sic contrarium omni Christiano quomodo crapula*

("There is nothing as out of place in a Christian as excess")

St. Benedict

St. Benedict mentions this in his Rule when speaking of the quantity of food that should be served the monk. He also adds a quote from Our Lord who said: "But take heed to yourselves lest your hearts be weighed down with dissipation and drunkenness and cares of this life, and that day come upon you suddenly like a snare" (Luke 21:34-35).

The Christian is to be ever vigilant and not weighed down by earthly cares. If we live as though everything depends upon the joy we feel at the present moment, our eyes are not then set on the joy that awaits us in heaven. Earthly food and drink fill us for a moment but leave us with hunger and thirst later. The Christian is called to a banquet where the Lord feeds us with the Bread of Life and slakes our thirst forever.

The person who eats and drinks in excess acts as though his very life depends upon this meal. When we realize that our very lives depend upon Our Lord and not the passing meal, we may find ourselves fasting instead of feasting. ‡

## *Nimia indulgentia corrumpit hominem*

("Too much indulgence corrupts")

TRADITIONAL

Life is difficult.

Parents who try to shield their children from that truth make an enormous mistake. As much as they would like to, they can't protect their children forever. Pain will find them sooner or later. If they've hidden them from difficulty, they've not given them the opportunity to develop the strength they'll need when their time comes.

Jesus didn't come to make life easy. He came to make us great. To love someone is to will to the person that which is good for the person and to provide that good if one is able. Giving in time after time is not good for one we claim to love. We teach the false lesson that everything will always go the way he or she wants it. It won't of course, and then we've given nothing but a future of total frustration.

None of us wants hardship, nor should we intentionally seek it out for its own sake. Nor should pleasure be our goal. Pleasure passes. God lasts. When we nurture temperance, we understand the purpose and limitation of this world's goods and we put them in their proper place: after God, who never fails. ‡

## *Quod oculus non videt cor non desiderat*

("What the eye doesn't see,
the heart won't want")

TRADITIONAL

We don't hear much talk today about protecting ourselves from the "occasion" of sin. The truth is that the path of holiness is much smoother if we ourselves do not encumber it by designing our own obstacles along the path.

Our Lord remarked: "Every one who looks at a woman lustfully has already committed adultery with her in his heart" (Matthew 5:28). Much is often made about the act of lust in the passage, but little is made of the act of looking. If we take custody of our eyes and guard what comes before us, we may well avoid the temptation to dwell on what our eyes present to us as fodder for sin.

We often are good about turning our eyes away from those in need while at the same time focusing on that which promises to fulfill our needs or imagined ones. Focusing our eyes on the cross of Christ will correct our vision and help us to see what is really important in life. ‡

## *Durum et durum non faciunt murum*

("Hard with hard never made any good wall")

ERASMUS

We know that a wall can't be built just of stones. There has to be something to hold it together, something pliable enough to mold itself into the shape of the stone and keep it firm.

Knowing when to be firm and knowing when to be gentle is a gift rooted in the willingness to be quiet and to discern what the moment calls for. We've all been in the room when two hardheaded debaters have been going at it: They never get anywhere.

Life is fluid. In an instant of anger, our instincts may propel us to shout and pronounce many harsh words. But with temperance, our instincts do not control us. Looking at the situation with the eyes of faith — which means, as much as possible, God's eyes — we put the brakes on those immediate reactions and consider what needs to be said, rather than what we'd like to say at the moment. The first message of the Beatitudes that Our Lord gave is to check your immediate reaction. ‡

## *Loqui ignorabit, qui tacere nesciet*

("The one who doesn't know how to hold his tongue knows not how to talk")

AUSONIUS

Talking should come from thought, and thought has to be quiet before it expresses itself. The Word of God says, "Out of the abundance of the heart, the mouth speaks" (Matthew 12:34).

Speaking is one thing, babbling is another.

Conveying a message is one thing, making noise is another.

Benedict says, "It befits the student to listen and learn. It befits the master to speak and teach."

When we hold our tongue, we can be listening. When we quiet our own desire to speak, we can pay attention to what others have to say. And only then do we grow in knowledge and, as a consequence, have something worth saying ourselves.

In the life of the spirit, the same rule applies. We spend a great deal of time talking to God. How much time do we spend listening to Him? ‡

*Qui immoderate omnia cupiunt, saepe in totum frustrantur*

("The one who grasps at too much holds nothing fast")

TRADITIONAL

We see it all the time: A child tries to wrap his arms around too many toys, and as a result, loses every one.

We try to save ourselves time by making one trip to the kitchen with all the dishes, and with one false step, they all come clattering down to the floor.

Temperance requires us to know our limits. There is only so much we can hold, so much we can do. Overreaching doesn't bring us closer; instead, it pushes us farther away from our goal.

In the spiritual life, we all want complete peace, and we want it now. We're frustrated because our knowledge of God is so limited. We want the ecstasy and inner peace of the saints, and are confused when we can't drive up to a window and order it.

Our desires need to be tempered, and our faith deepened. When we want more than we are able to have, we're expressing a distrust of God. In fact, we're saying that we know better than God what's good for us.

God knows what we need. He's offering it to us right this moment, as a matter of fact. Isn't it sad when our anxious desires and our intemperate greed push us away from God's embrace, and instead of gaining a little, we lose it all? ‡

## *Vinum apostatare facit etiam sapientes*

("Wine makes even the wisest go astray")

JESUS SIRACH (SIRACH 19:2)

St. Benedict quotes this verse from Sirach when he speaks about the quantity of drink a monk should be allowed. Benedict's preference is that the amount be less than would satiate the monk's thirst.

St. Paul says, "Do not be foolish, but understand what the will of the Lord is. And do not get drunk with wine, for that is debauchery, but be filled with the Spirit" (Ephesians 5:18-19). None of us is wise enough to overcome the temptations of the flesh, but we should be smart enough to know how much is too much.

Experience, either our own or the witness of others, tells us that when we are impaired we often do that which we would not if we were in control of our senses. Although impairment might mitigate our culpability for acts we commit while impaired, the culpability for choosing to become impaired remains ours.

Moderation in all things leads to virtue. The only thing we should ever hope to have in excess is God's Spirit. For everything else, *Satis . . . satis!* — "Enough is enough!" ‡

# Epilogus

(Epilogue)

*Vade in pace!*

("Go in peace!")

TRADITIONAL ROMAN FAREWELL

The Romans bid each other farewell with, *Vade in pace!* — "Go in peace!"

Since the renewal of the Liturgy we Catholics have grown accustomed to this farewell greeting, too. It is interesting to note that Our Lord's disciples would have been familiar with the Romans' use of this leave-taking message. It also clarifies Our Lord's farewell to them, "Peace I leave with you, my peace I give to you; not as the world gives do I give to you" (John 14:27). His peace is not the same as the everyday nicety the Romans exchanged routinely.

The few thoughts captured in these pages are meant to remind us through reading and reflection that the Lord's peace is heritage for every circumstance, no matter the happening. It's His gift along with — inseparable from — His cross. Dante caught it all: *In voluntate eius pax nostra*, "In His will is our peace."

These reflections also warn us that the theme song in hell may easily be: "I Did It My Way." The world sets before us one avenue of peace, the Lord another.

While life here is still ours, may we seek after His peace and pursue it. And then we'll know its fullness eternally.

As the Lord gives, not as the world, *Vade in pace!* ‡